AN ANTHOLOGY OF
THE LOVE OF GOD

EVELYN UNDERHILL

An Anthology of the
LOVE OF GOD

From the Writings of
EVELYN UNDERHILL

Edited by the Right Rev.
LUMSDEN BARKWAY, D.D.

and

LUCY MENZIES

DAVID McKAY COMPANY, INC.
New York

First published in 1953

PRINTED IN GREAT BRITAIN BY
A. R. MOWBRAY & CO. LIMITED IN THE CITY OF OXFORD
3206

WHEN the evening of this life comes we shall be judged on Love.

St. John of the Cross

THE mystics, to give them their short familiar name, are men and women who insist that they know for certain the presence and activity of that which they call the Love of God.

Evelyn Underhill

LIST OF CONTENTS

TABLE OF CONTENTS AND SOURCES

Where no source is given the extract has been taken from a periodical or from unpublished material

I. THE NATURE OF PURE LOVE

II. THE LOVE OF THE GODHEAD

I. GOD, THE SOURCE AND SUM OF LOVE

II. CHRIST, THE EVIDENCE AND PROOF OF LOVE

7

IV. THE SPIRITUAL LIFE

V. SANCTIFICATION, THE GROWTH IN LOVE

VI. PENITENCE, THE OUTCOME OF LOVE

VII. DISCIPLINE, THE TRAINING IN LOVE

VIII. SERVICE, THE ACTIVITY OF LOVE

ACKNOWLEDGEMENTS

BOTH on our own behalf and that of the publishers of this volume we should like to express our appreciation of the kindness of those responsible for the copyright of the late Evelyn Underhill's works in giving the requisite permissions. To Mrs. Gillian Wilkinson, the holder, grateful acknowledgement is made of her complete support: to the various publishers of Evelyn Underhill's books, as set forth below, fullest thanks are due for their ready and generous consent to the use of extracts on terms which make this anthology possible. In addition there are the extracts from unpublished material, and from essays in periodicals, the literary property of Mrs. Gillian Wilkinson, to acknowledge with special thanks to her. Lastly we wish to recognize, with the fullest possible appreciation, the kind help of Dr. Margaret Reid, Hilda Francis, Patience Mackenzie, Joyce McMaster, and Phyllis Potter, in looking out and preparing the material from which the final selection was made.

We are indebted to the following publishers for copyright material from their publications:

Methuen & Co. Ltd., for: *Mysticism; The Golden Sequence; The Life of the Spirit; Mixed Pasture; The House of the Soul; Concerning the Inner Life; Man and the Supernatural.*

Longmans Green & Co. Ltd., for: *The Fruits of the Spirit;*

Abba; The Mystery of Sacrifice; The Light of Christ; The School of Charity; Letters; Meditations and Prayers.

J. M. Dent & Sons Ltd., for: *The Mystic Way; Practical Mysticism; The Essentials of Mysticism; Immanence; Theophanies.*

G. Bell & Sons Ltd., for *Ruysbroeck.*

James Nisbet & Co. Ltd., for *Worship.*

Hodder & Stoughton Ltd., for *The Spiritual Life.*

LUMSDEN BARKWAY, *Bishop*
LUCY MENZIES

July, 1953

INTRODUCTION

IF the fashion of autobiography became even more wide-spread than it is, and more people imitated Marcus Aurelius in the pious tributes of affectionate gratitude which make up the first chapter of his famous soliloquies, it might be surprising to find in how many cases the name of Evelyn Underhill appeared. She has been dead twelve years. Her books are never advertised, and yet they go on having a steady sale. With some notable writers of our own day their death seemed almost the end of their reputation. But Evelyn Underhill still exerts a potent influence. If those who feel themselves her debtors were further to imitate Marcus Aurelius by specifying the essential cause of their gratitude, the answer might very well be the title chosen for this anthology. What greater gift could one give to another than reassurance on this fundamental issue? This, to many people, as it was to Bishop Gore, is the most difficult of all dogmas, yet it is the one above all others about which they long to reach certitude.

The eminent Victorian, F. W. H. Myers, in a group of other eminent Victorians, uttered the cry of all hearts, when he said that if he were allowed to put one question to the Sphinx, with the certainty of getting an infallible answer, he would ask, 'Is the universe friendly?' In other words, Is the Power behind it Love? In the consulting-room of a Harley Street psychiatrist one patient is reported to have said, 'Make me sure that there is a God of Love and I shall go away a well man.' There are many who will understand the story of the austere and dour Hebrew scholar, 'Rabbi' Duncan, renowned far beyond his university of Aberdeen for his learning, who recalled in an unusual moment of expansiveness, the ecstasy that came on him when his youthful doubts were resolved and God's Love became clear: 'When I knew there was a God, I danced upon the Brig o' Dee with delight.'

Evelyn Underhill's faith was not more easily come by than his; and it is both the thrill and the conviction in her voice which hearten the wistful seeker in his quest. The way in which she always speaks about God, with the wide perspective of her scholarship, the stern integrity of her thought, the analytic clearness of her disciplined mind, and the devout awe of her heart, reassures the reader that here is a witness whom he can trust because she has taken nothing for granted and speaks out of the fullness of personal exploration and experience.

For genius there is no accounting. Heredity and environment do not explain it. And Evelyn Underhill's testimony may mean more to the matter-of-fact person because neither her heredity nor environment was in the least remarkable. The profession of her father and her husband was that of the law; and it was in the dry, keen, tonic atmosphere of legal acuteness and wit that she habitually lived. Her early church-going, such as it was, seems to have been conventional. 'I was not brought up to religion,' she said. She obviously took herself seriously, for there remains a record of her self-scrutiny in her fifteenth year. Little, however, though she knew it, her mind was being trained for her life-work. Her educational privileges were great, though not on stereotyped lines. Because of their variety they helped her 'to see life steadily, and to see it whole.' She was a diligent student at King's College, London; and there, and elsewhere, she attended courses in English and continental history, in science and art; and went to classes in ambulance work, cookery, carpentering, bookbinding, and other useful activities. Thus her mind was being trained to exercise itself skilfully and efficiently in the pursuit of philosophy and theology, which, later on, turned out to be the true field in which to expend her fullest powers, and in which she was self-taught. She never ceased researching; she never ceased learning. Hers was that 'suppleness' of mind that seemed to her such an important possession; with the result that after her death when *The Times Literary Supplement* summed up her achievement, the writer, choosing his words with care, said that she possessed 'an insight into the meaning both of the culture and of the individual gropings of the soul that was unmatched by any of the professional teachers of her day.' In all this steady progress one may perceive, without being taunted with pious credulity, the unobtrusive guiding of the Divine Love.

We have not much material for tracing the steps of her spiritual development. In the three novels which were her earliest literary work there are patent indications that she had submitted to the lure of the Supernatural; and in 1907 (which was also the year of her marriage) a distinct occurrence took place which she called her 'conversion.' By now she was beginning to collect material for her classic book on Mysticism, which appeared in 1911, by which she became famous to an ever-widening public. Hints of the point of view she had then reached may be found in her two 'John Cordelier' books. Further stages in her progress may be marked by her friendship with von Hügel, by whom she was very greatly influenced, as even the phraseology of her books bears evidence. He contributed to her training in love, not only for God but also for His poor; and it may be that the altruistic side of her spiritual life, of which we have such clear evidence in the seventeenth section of the Anthology, owes not a little to his teaching. By it she was inspired to undertake systematic visiting not less than two afternoons a week in the slums of North

Kensington. She lived intensely in two worlds, the Hither as well as the Yonder, for both are really one; and love without service and sacrifice was to her an impossibility.

Through von Hügel, also, her religion became increasingly Christo-centric. Previous to that (before 1923-4) she said, 'I had never had any personal experience of our Lord.' After that she would have insisted in the strongest possible way on the rightness of the heading for the third section of the Anthology: the Incarnation is the only ultimate proof of the Divine Love.

A further stage may be noted, with deep respect and something approaching to awe, but also with grateful reassurance of spirit. Evelyn Underhill was not to be allowed to evade the final testing of love. She was still more fully to realize for herself, and reveal to us, that the Way of Love is inevitably the Way of the Cross. She knew at first hand what the mystics tell of the apparent hiding of God's face and the Dark Night of the Soul. In her last great book, *Worship*, come the tremendous words, 'Worship is summed up in sacrifice.' They were wrung from her heart. She had penetrated into the innermost 'mystery' (in the proper sense of the word 'mystery') of the Christian life, hidden in bygone ages but now advertised for ever on Calvary. The 'flame of the Everlasting Love' can not only warm and enlighten: it 'must burn till it transform.' Charles Williams speaks of this, and quotes her own words in his Introduction to her *Letters*; further than this we must not presume to intrude. It is enough for us to know that she accepted the final test, and emerged triumphant, unshaken in her assurance of the triumph of Love.

II

Some one has spoken of her sanctity. She has spoken of various types of sanctity. 'Holiness, the perfect correspondence of the human soul with the Eternal, takes as many forms as human character itself . . . For, in truth, the vocation of the saint is a call to the heroic levels of existence; and in whatever way this call is obeyed it casts an unbecoming light on that which the Abbé Huvelin was accustomed to call our "incurable mediocrity of soul".' Her holiness was of the type which hid itself in the apparent 'ordinariness' of her outward life. Coventry Patmore might have had Evelyn Underhill in mind when he wrote his famous description of a saint, of which the chief note is unostentatiousness:

I have known two or three such persons, and I declare that . . . I should never have guessed that they were any wiser or better than myself, or any ordinary man of the world with a prudent regard for the common proprieties. I once asked a person, more learned than I am in such matters, to tell me what was the real difference. The reply was that the saint does everything that any other decent person does, only somewhat better and with a totally different motive.

Certainly Evelyn Underhill did most things 'somewhat better': she was expert and efficient to a degree; and all things were done with one motive, the Divine Love. She herself has expressed the 'difference' in words which cannot be bettered:

Those who have most deeply reflected have perceived that the change effected is not a change of worlds. It is rather such a change of temper and attitude as will disclose within our one world, here and now, the one Spirit in the diversity of His gifts; the one Love, in homeliest incidents as well as noblest vision, laying its obligations on the soul; and so the true nature and full possibilities of this our present life. (*Life of the Spirit*, p. 25.)

Within our one world, here and now, she lived the double life, of Martha and Mary, not withdrawn in cloistered calm, but fulfilling the incessant claims made on her as the wife of a busy professional man, keeping house and acting as hostess in the West End of London, doing her sick and poor visiting, lecturing and addressing public meetings; and

at the same time leading her 'secret' (because sacred) life,
hid with Christ in God, in the unhurried and exacting
intimacies of prayer.

From quite early days she had been consulted on matters
of spiritual direction, and in the end her correspondence
assumed most exhausting proportions. It increased enormously after 1924 when she became known as a Retreat
conductor and also a theological lecturer. We are greatly
enriched by having the reports of several of these activities
in some of her best-known books, in which the solid learning
of her larger volumes is put into more readily assimilable
form, with a wealth of homely illustration and metaphor.

What impressed people was her serenity. Doubtless,
once again, love was the explanation of all this. Despite
her physical fragility (how often was it said, 'It seemed as if
a breath would blow her away!') she achieved an amount of
labour that it is difficult to credit. But holiness is another
form of wholeness, for which another word is Salvation
(*salus*, health) as she and many others have pointed out.

No one can read with attention the Gospels and the story of the
primitive Church, without being struck by the consciousness of
renovation, of enhancement, experienced by all who received the
Christian secret . . . Everything goes to prove that the 'more abundant
life' offered by the Johannine Christ to His followers, was literally
experienced by them; and was the source of their joy, their enthusiasm,
their mutual love and power of endurance' (*Life of the Spirit*, p. 44).

Love is always an energy; and the greater the love the
greater its power. It was not a weak or emaciated body
on which our Lord 'bore our sins to the Tree.'

She knew also how to husband her resources: true holiness
includes wisdom. If the bow is to be efficient it must not be
always bent. From childhood she had always been accustomed to good holidays, with her father on his yacht and
her mother in continental travel. (The present writer

came across her name long before it was known to the public, in a short and graphic description of Verona, for which she had gained a prize in the pages of *The Academy* in 1900 or 1901.) In 1922 she wrote a semi-humorous letter to *John o'London's Weekly* which discloses more than it actually declares:

My ideal holiday would be spent in a mountainous district, preferably within sight of snow, and as far as possible from roads and railways. The plants must be varied and interesting, the animals friendly, the human beings inconspicuous. For its full enjoyment, a very short skirt, very thick nailed boots, and a loose coat with two pockets, are needed. One pocket contains poetry and binoculars; the other sandwiches, and, later in the day, botanical specimens. The companion for such a holiday requires most careful selection, and must possess a sympathetic eye for simple beauty, some capacity for silence, and no craving whatever for intelligent conversation.

Accounts of early holidays, with vivid word-painting and pencil drawings, taken from her diaries are to be found in the delightful posthumous volume, *Shrines and Cities of France and Italy*. They show how keen were her perceptions and how wide her culture.

III

'Finding and expressing love': that phrase sums it all up. If you want a concise statement of her 'world-view,'—her clue to the baffling queerness of things which constitutes human existence,—you will find it in two lines of William Blake, to whom she was so fond of referring:

And we are put on earth a little space
That we may learn to bear the beams of love.

Love is all its meaning. What she understood by Love is plain in the quotations which make up this volume. To her it was identical with 'Reality,' the word which she used constantly in her earlier volumes. In *Practical Mysticism* she gave this definition of Mysticism: 'Mysticism is the art of union with Reality. The mystic is a person who has attained that union in greater or lesser degree; or who aims at and believes in such attainment.' Towards this difficult and costly art the Divine Love had been directing her from the beginning. It is significant that when she was asked to name the books which had most influenced her she mentioned (a) St. Augustine's *Confessions*, whose theme is the pursuit and strategy of Love; (b) Plotinus, who speaks of 'this Indwelling Love as no other than the Spirit which walks with every being, the affection dominant in each several nature' (*Ennead III*). (c) Dante's *Paradiso*, which describes the culmination and victory of the Love which 'moves the sun and all the stars'; and (d) von Hügel's *Mystical Element of Religion*, which describes and analyses the personality of one to whom life and love were identical. All these writers initiated her more deeply into that experience which is called 'mystical', which all her books are an attempt to expound. She herself was a mystic (though she modestly deprecated the name); but very definitely a Christian mystic. As a philosopher she rejected Monism as an explanation of Reality, and from the point of view of this Anthology the reason is important: Monism leaves no room for love. There is a most illuminating letter which she wrote to *The Spectator* after the publication of *Man and the Supernatural* (one of the most important of her smaller books, though its circulation had been disastrously affected by an impossibly jejune review in a church paper) which it is well worth while disinterring here so that it may not be entirely lost. Her aim in writing that book

was to set out a philosophy of religion able to give content to all the characteristic experiences and activities of man's spiritual life: its outward and inward, its historical and metaphysical aspects. Such a philosophy must be based on the fundamental distinction between Creator and creature . . . Monistic mysticism simply does not give content to these observed facts of the spiritual life. It means a view of reality which is indistinguishable from pantheism: an immanentism so extreme that both prayer and worship become meaningless. An even more serious defect is that such a 'mysticism' leaves no place for love.

. . . . .

More than once she quotes with approval the saying of St. John of the Cross, 'When the evening of this life comes we shall be judged on Love.' This sums up her message. The difficulty in this anthology is not what to put in, but what to leave out. All her books are variations of this central theme. The selections show what she wished to signify by that most misused word, not a gentle and pleasant emotion, but a tremendous and sometimes terrifying force. In face of that supreme Reality sentimentalism is one of the most insidious foes of Christianity, and self-complacency, perhaps, its deadliest sin. Love is the cosmic energy that flames from the constellations and is concealed in the abyss of the atom; is whispered by the Holy Spirit in the heart, and placarded before men's eyes upon the Cross. It offers to us all that it has, and demands from us all that we can give. Of these august truths Evelyn Underhill reminds us in the pages which follow. In making the selection we have been guided by words of commendation which she herself gave to a volume of readings from Baron von Hügel: 'All the extracts are of substantial length; there are no "snippets", no mere "fine sayings".' And we hope the same verdict may be passed on this volume as she passed on that: 'It should give countless readers a true initiation into [her] rich and closely woven thought. . . .'. It contains 'the very essence of its great author's love and wisdom, and offers to those willing to accept it the real and costly food of eternal life.'

LUMSDEN BARKWAY
Bishop

I

THE NATURE OF PURE LOVE

STIGMATA

Must I be wounded in the untiring feet
That hasted all the way
My Dear to greet?
Shall errant love endure this hard delay,
Limping and slow
On its ascents to go?
    Yea this must be
    If thou would'st come with Me:
    Thus only can
    My seal be set on man.

Must I be wounded in the busy hands
That labour to fulfil
Industrious love's demands
Within the circle of thy sovereign will?
And can it fall within that will to let
Thy child from all repayment of its debt?
    Yea, this must be
    If thou would'st work for Me:
    Thus only can
    My seal be set on man.

And is it thus? then gladly I go lame,
Bring nought within my hands save this thy sign:
See, I exult! all bliss is in the flame
That mars, yet brands me thine.
Thine are my members: strike again and give
A deeper, sweeter hurt, that dying I may live.
    Yea, this must be
    Since I would live to thee:
    Thus only can
    Thy seal be set on man.

Make thou thy blazon perfect; let my heart
The piercing wound of thy swift love receive,
That only cunning lance which hath the art
Man's sickness to relieve.
Make the place deep and wide,
That thou may'st find a nook wherein to hide:
    For this must be,
    And thou shalt dwell in me.
    Thus only can
    Thy seal be set on man.

LOVE AND DESIRE

LOVE: that over-worked and ill-used word, often confused on the one hand with passion and on the other with amiability. If we ask the most fashionable sort of psychologist what love is, he says that it is the impulse urging us towards that end which is the fulfilment of any series of deeds or 'behaviour-cycle'; the psychic thread on which all the apparently separate actions making up that cycle are strung and united. In this sense love need not be fully conscious, to reach the level of feeling; but it *must* be an imperative, inward urge. And if we ask those who have known and taught the life of the Spirit, they too say that love is a passionate tendency, an inward vital urge of the soul towards its Source; which impels every living thing to pursue the most profound trend of its being, reaches consciousness in the form of self-giving and of desire, and its only satisfying goal in God. Love is for them much more than its emotional manifestations. It is 'the ultimate cause of the true activities of all active things'—no less.

LOVE AND RESPONSE

Pure Love or Charity—utter self-giving which is our reply to the Love of God—is the same as sanctity. What is pure love? That which gives and gives and never demands. In the words of Gertrude More: *Courageous, humble, constant: not worn out with labours, not daunted by difficulties*—bravely sticking it out when tired, disheartened, worried. And to do this, we look beyond it all, trying to respond to the Love of God, seeking and serving Christ in our fellow-men. If we do that faithfully, give ourselves to

God's purposes, we will develop such depth of peaceful, devoted love as passes beyond the need of being fed by feeling or the consolations of religion—the chocolate creams of the Christian life. Do not make the mistake of thinking if you feel cold and dead, that you do not know how to love.

LOVE AND WILL

To love God, without demand or measure, in and for Himself—this is Charity: and Charity is the spiritual life. Only this most gently powerful of all attractions and all pressures can capture and purify the will of man and subordinate it to the great purpose of God; for as His Love and Will are One, so the love and will of man must become one. Therefore all other purifications, disciplines and practices have meaning because they prepare and contribute to the invasion and transformation of the heart by the uncreated Charity of God. 'Thou art the Love wherewith the heart loves Thee.'

For it is only when the secret thrust of our whole being is thus re-ordered by God and set towards God, that peace is established in the house of life. Then the disorderly energies of emotion and will are rectified and harmonized, and all the various and wide-spreading love which we pour out towards other souls and things is deepened, unselfed and made safe; because that which is now sought and loved in them is the immanent Divine thought and love. Thus the will transformed in Charity everywhere discovers God. It sees behind and within even the most unpleasing creatures the all-pleasing Creator, and loves and cherishes in and for Him, that which in itself, never could be loved. It discerns and adores His mysterious action within the most homely activities and most disconcerting frustrations

of the common life. And by this glad recognition of that
secret Presence, all the apprehensions of the senses, all the
conceivings of the mind, all the hoarded treasures and
experiences of the past, are cleansed and sanctified.

LOVE AND SELF-ABANDONMENT

'The proper work of the will is to love God.' The
relentless drive of our nature towards an undiscerned and
yet desired fulfilment can have no other end: and in so far
as it has departed from this, its only adequate objective,
and has frittered its energies on half-real objects of desire,
its aim must be corrected by the pressure of Reality.

Rege quod est devium.[1]

In proportion to our haunting intuition of the Perfect,
will be the ceaseless disillusionments which follow our
attempt to find and enjoy that Perfect, embodied in the
imperfect satisfactions of the temporal world. In so far
as we try to rest in them, even the holy incarnations and
sacramental actions of religion baffle while they enchant us:
for they do not quench but stimulate our metaphysical
craving and point beyond themselves to that all-cherishing,
all-penetrating Loveliness which makes them lovely, and
can only be known by us in the self-abandonment of love.

O Lux beatissima,
Reple cordis intima
Tuorum fidelium.[2]

[1] Bring back the wandering.
[2] O Light most blessed
Fill the heart's deep
Of all who confess Thee.

THE PASSION OF LOVE

It is not easy to disentangle will and feeling; for in all intense will there is a strong element of emotion—every volitional act has somewhere at the back of it a desire—and in all great and energizing passions there is a pronounced volitional element. The 'synthesis of love and will' is no mere fancy of the psychologist. It is a compound hard to break down in practice. But I think we can say generally that the business of feeling is to inflame the will, to give it intention, gladness and vividness; to convert it from a dull determination into an eager, impassioned desire. It links up thought and action; effects in psychological language, the movement of the prayerful self from a mere state of cognition to a state of conation; converts the soul from attention to the Transcendent to first-hand adventure within it. 'All thy life now behoveth altogether to stand in desire,' says the author of the *Cloud of Unknowing* to the disciple who has accepted the principle of prayer; and here he is declaring a psychological necessity rather than a religious platitude, for all successful action has its origin in emotion of some kind. Though we choose to imagine that 'pure reason' directs our conduct, in the last resort we always do a thing because of the feeling that we have about it. Not necessarily because we like doing it; but because instinctive feeling of some sort—selfish or unselfish, personal, social, conventional, sacrificial; the disturbing emotion called the sense of duty, or the glorious emotion called the passion of love—is urging us to it.

LOVE, THE LIFE-GIVING LIFE

It is Love which breaks down the barrier between finite and infinite life. But Love, as he (Ruysbroeck) understands

it, has little in common with the feeling-state to which
many of the female mystics have given that august name.
For him, it is hardly an emotional word at all, and never
a sentimental one; rather the title of a mighty force, a
holy energy that fills the universe—the essential activity
of God. Sometimes he describes it under the antique
imagery of Light; imagery which is more than a metaphor,
and is connected with that veritable consciousness of enhanced radiance, as well in the outer as in the inner world,
experienced by the 'illuminated' mystic.

Again it is the 'life-giving Life,' hidden in God and the
substance of our souls, which the self finds and appropriates;
the whole Johannine trilogy brought into play, to express
its meaning for heart, intellect and will. This Love, in fact,
is the dynamic power which St. Augustine compared with
gravitation, 'drawing all things to their own place,' and
which Dante saw binding the multiplicity of the universe
into one. All Ruysbroeck's images for it turn on the idea of
force. It is a raging fire, a storm, a flood. He speaks of it
in one great passage as 'playing like lightning' between God
and the soul.

LOVE, THE SEED OF GOOD

'The fruit of the Spirit,' says St. Paul, 'is Love, Joy, Peace,
Long-Suffering, Gentleness, Goodness, Faithfulness, Meekness, Temperance'—all the things the world most needs. . . . I
do not think St. Paul arranged his list of the fruits of the
Spirit in a casual order. They represent a progressive series
from one point, and that one point is Love, the living,
eternal seed from which all grow. We all know that
Christians are baptized 'into a life summed up in love,'
even though we have to spend the rest of our own lives
learning how to do it. Love, therefore, is the budding-point

from which all the rest come: that tender, cherishing attitude; that unlimited self-forgetfulness, generosity and kindness which is the attitude of God to all His creatures; and so must be the attitude towards them which His Spirit brings forth in us. . . . To be unloving is to be out of touch with God. So the generous, cherishing Divine Love, the indiscriminate delight in others, just or unjust, must be our model too. To come down to brass tacks, God loves the horrid man at the fish shop, and the tiresome woman in the next flat, and the disappointing Vicar . . . and the contractor who has cut down the row of trees we loved, to build a row of revolting bungalows. God *loves*, not tolerates, these wayward, half-grown, self-centred spirits, and seeks without ceasing to draw them into His love. And the first-fruit of His indwelling presence, the first sign that we are on His side and He on ours, must be at least a tiny bud of this Charity breaking the hard and rigid outline of our life.

LOVE AND ITS SEQUENCE

The Fruit of the Spirit is Love, Joy, Peace—that three-fold formula of blessedness. . . .

First comes Love, Charity, pure, undemanding, generous love of God in Himself and of His creatures, good and bad, congenial and uncongenial, for His sake; a certain share in His generous, loving action, the way He cares for all life. Each Christian soul who learns that in prayer and teaches it in everyday life, has made a contribution to the peace of the world. He who loveth not, knoweth not God. In hard, ungenerous hearts, the Spirit cannot grow and increase. We can understand that bit even though we cannot always practise it. But then St. Paul suddenly ascends to the very summit of the spirit and says, not that the spirit of love shall bring forth such suitable qualities as penitence, diligence, helpfulness, unworldliness, good social and religious habits, but that the real sign that God, the Giver of Life, has been received into our souls will be joy and peace: joy, the spirit of selfless delight; peace, the spirit of tranquil acceptance; the very character of the beatitude of Heaven, given here and *now* in our grubby little souls, provided only that they are loving little souls. If, in spite of all conflicts, weakness, sufferings, sins, we open our door, the spirit is poured out within us and the first mark of its presence is not an increase of energy but joy and peace.

We should not have guessed that. Yet real love always heals fear and neutralizes egotism, and so, as love grows up in us, we shall worry about ourselves less and admire and delight in God and His other children more and more, and this is the secret of joy. We shall no longer strive for our own way, but commit ourselves easily and simply to God's way, acquiesce in His will and in so doing find our peace.

LOVE: DONATION AND DEMAND

Love is a grave and ruthless passion, unlimited in self-giving and unlimited in demand.

THE FINAL OBJECT OF LOVE

Here, then, reason and love combine to assure us that our end is God alone; first realized as an influence, one amongst other claims and objects of desire, and then, as we more and more respond to His attraction, as the only satisfaction of the heart; and at last as the all-penetrating, all-compelling Reality, that only Life which is recognized by Faith, desired in Hope, achieved by Charity. Then all these separate movements of love and longing—those passionate self-givings and agonies of desire—in which the struggling and half-awakened spirit reaches out towards life and draws back to the prison of solitary pain, find their solution and satisfaction in God; and there is established in her that steadfast habitude of love which makes her the open channel and docile instrument of the one Divine Love. 'Who dwelleth in Charity dwelleth in God and God in him': for the secret of Charity is an opening up of the whole tangled, many-levelled creature to the penetration of that Spirit which already indwells the soul's ground.

II

THE LOVE OF THE GODHEAD

GOD, THE SOURCE AND SUM OF LOVE

DYNAMIC LOVE

Not to me
The Unmoved Mover of philosophy
And absolute still sum of all that is,
The God whom I adore—not this!
Nay, rather a great moving wave of bliss,
A surging torrent of dynamic love
In passionate swift career,
That down the sheer
And fathomless abyss
Of Being ever pours, his ecstasy to prove.

As the glad river's life
More glad becomes in music of much strife,
So does that spiritual flood
Dashed in full song,
In quick stupendous majesty of joy
The oppositions of the world among,
Come to fair crest in every breaking bud:
Yea, can the very conflict's self employ
A coloured spray of loveliness to fling
Athwart the world-wide landscape on the wing
Of every flying thing.

Dynamic love glints gay on the plume's tip
Of fat and restless wrens, tears at the heart
From the divine and vibrant bramble wreathes
That mesh the hedge with beauty. It out-breathes

Fragrance of pure surrender in the smart
Of sacrificial hay-fields. On the lip
Of frail ecstatic poppies it brims up,
As flaming meditations in the soul
Drowsed with deep passion. E'en the narrow cup
Of inconspicuous verve in still the strange
And awful tincture to fulfilment brings:
There doth my Dear pursue his chemic art,
And thence distils the magic of the whole.
For Love is time, succession, ardour, change;
It is the holy thrust of living things
That seek a consummation and enlace
Some fragment of the All in each fecund embrace
Whence life again flows forth upon its endless chase.

Love ever moves, yet love eternal is;
Love ever seeks, yet seeks itself to find;
And, all-surrendered to the leman's kiss,
Doth but itself with its own passion bind.
O sacred, ceaseless flow!
O wondrous meeting
Of the unchanging and the ever-fleeting,
That still by the sad way of sorriest lust
Confers a secret glory on the teeming dust.
See! by love's loss we find ourselves indeed,
See! the world's death the world's true life doth feed,
And Love dynamic to Love's rest doth go.

MOUNTAIN FLORA

As the plant on the smooth of the hill
That sees not the deep and the height,
That knows not the might
Of the whole—

I am rooted and grounded in him,
The small leaves of my soul
Thrust up from his will

I know not the terrible peak,
The white and ineffable Thought,
Whence the hill-torrents flow
And my nurture is brought.
I am little and meek;
I dare not to lift
My look to his snow,
But drink, drop by drop, of its gift.

Some say, on the face
Of that ultimate height
Small plants have their place:
Rapt far from our sight
In the solitude strange
Where the infinite dream mounts range beyond range
To the infinite sky, there they grow.

Where the intellect faints
In the silence and cold,
There, humble and glad, their petals unfold.
As the innocent bell
Of the Least Soldanella thrusts up through the snow,
So the hearts of the saints
On the terrible height of the Godhead may dwell;
Held safe by the Will
As we, on the smooth of the hill.

(THESE are) four ways among the many in which the human creature experiences the fact of God and God is disclosed to men. . . .

First, in History we find the Supernatural penetrating Process and revealed through it.

Next, in Incarnation—and, depending from this, in the fact of sanctity—we find the Supernatural penetrating Personality and revealed through it.

Thirdly, in Sacraments and Symbols, we find the Supernatural penetrating created Things, and revealed to the soul through the channels of sense.

Last, in Prayer we find the Supernatural in immediate contact with created spirit; self-revealed within the Individual Soul.

REVELATION

That which we really know about God is not what we have been clever enough to find out, but what the Divine Charity has secretly revealed.

INDWELLING AND ALL-PERVADING LOVE

What, then, is the nature of that Eternal God, the Substance of all that is, so far as we are able to apprehend Him? . . .

God is Love: or rather Charity; generous, outflowing, self-giving love, *Agape*. When all the qualities which human thought attributes to Reality are set aside, this remains. Charity is the colour of the Divine personality, the spectrum of holiness. We believe that the tendency of give, to share, to cherish, is the mainspring of the universe, ultimate cause of all that is, and reveals the Nature of God: and therefore that when we are most generous we are most living and most real . . . To enter the Divine order then, achieve the full life for which we are made, means entering an existence which only has meaning as the channel and expression of an infinite, self-spending love . . . When we look out towards this Love that moves the stars and stirs in the child's heart and claims our total allegiance, and remember that this alone is Reality and we are only real so far as we conform to its demands, we see our human situation from a fresh angle; and perceive that it is both more humble and dependent, and more splendid, than we had dreamed. We are surrounded and penetrated by great spiritual forces of which we hardly know anything. Yet the outward events of our life cannot be understood, except in their relation to that unseen and intensely living world, the Infinite Charity which penetrates and supports us, the God whom we resist and yet for whom we thirst; who is ever at work, transforming the self-centred desire of the natural creature into the wide-spreading, outpouring love of the citizen of Heaven.

SELF-YIELDING TO ETERNAL LOVE

The Light, Life and Love of God—which are all the same thing really—are aspects of His Being, His Living Presence, and will be disclosed . . . to each soul according to its capacity and need. Let us try to see our situation in that large and general way: our small imperfect souls, waiting here on the Eternal God already fully present in His splendour; and His living Spirit which is His Love, gradually penetrating and fertilizing all our lives; reaching into and transforming the most humble activities of those lives, making them what God wants them to be. 'Remember,' said the Abbé de Tourville, 'that God loves your soul, not in some aloof, impersonal way, but passionately, with the adoring cherishing love of a parent for a child. The outpouring of His Holy Spirit is really the outpouring of His love, surrounding and penetrating your little soul with a peaceful, joyful delight in His creature: tolerant, peaceful love full of long-suffering and gentleness, working quietly, able to wait for results, faithful, devoted, without variableness or shadow of turning. Such is the charity of God' . . .

Love breaks down the barrier that shuts most of us from Heaven. That thought is too much for us really, yet it is the central truth of the spiritual life. And that loving, self-yielding to the Eternal Love—that willingness that God shall possess, indwell, fertilize, bring forth the fruit of *His* Spirit in us, instead of the fruits of *our* spirit—is the secret of all Christian power and Christian peace.

THE BROODING SPIRIT OF GOD

In the beginning God created the heaven and the earth. And the Earth was without form and void: and darkness was upon the face of the deep; and the Spirit of God was brooding on the face of the waters.

Let us consider this picture which comes to us from the great Biblical poem of the Creation. Darkness, chaos, mystery: and yet, already manifest, the first of all energies and actions, the cherishing, loving action of God. Love that hopes all and does all, brooding on the formless, unpromising deeps.

Beyond the ceaseless movement, the flaming sun, the vast spaces of the material universe, as science shows it to us, the Poet of the Universe, the Creative Spirit of God, brooding, with the patient, fostering action of love, on His restless, unformed, chaotic, empty world. And the author of the passage in Genesis does not see those dark waters, that chaos lashed by spiritual action into great waves.

It is not the dreadful energy and infinite space of the stellar universe which strike him first. He takes us beyond all that and shows us the world as it comes into being under the action of the Thought of God—Brooding. The true majesty of the Creative Action is manifest in its quietness. Bit by bit, the tranquil, brooding Spirit draws forth their latent possibilities, the beauty, wonder, variety of life.

So the great Thinker broods unhurried on His material, as a great musician on a theme, till the moment of creation comes, and life, truth and beauty appear. But really that long, brooding, quiet, when nothing seems to happen— the mind and will intent on that which is to be, when all is still, without form and void—*this* is part and a great part of the action of Creation. Here 'the Holy Ghost over the bent world broods.' Here the Eternal Artist, Eternal Love, is at work.

So we dwell on this great picture of Creation, lying under the warm shadow of His wings: the quietness of the dark waters, those mysterious deeps with all their unrealized possibilities of life, beauty and power—and the patient, loving presence of God, the Perfect, Who, by His ceaseless action on the imperfect, alone gives form and brings forth life. We are not looking on something finished and done with; we look, so far as we dare, at an Eternal process—the increasing action of the Divine Love.

The world in which we now are, from one point of view so lovely, from another so chaotic, unharmonizing, turbulent, so far from fulfilling the intention of God. The Holy Ghost *now* broods over the bent world: giving form to the formless, life to the lifeless, bringing form, beauty, significance, holiness; creating from chaos the Kingdom of God.

OUR FATHER AND HOME

God, Who stands so decisively over against our life, the Source of all splendour and all joy, is yet in closest and most cherishing contact with us; and draws us, beyond all splendour and joy, into Truth. He has created in us such a craving for Himself alone, that even the brief flashes of Eternity which sometimes visit us make all else seem dust and ashes, lifeless and unreal. Hence there should be no situation in our life, no attitude, no pre-occupation or relationship, from which we cannot look up to this God of absolute Truth and say 'Our Father,' of ourselves and of all other souls involved. Our inheritance *is* God, our Father and Home. We recognize Him, says St. John of the Cross, because we already carry in our hearts a rough sketch of the beloved countenance. Looking into these deeps, as into a quiet pool in the dark forest, we there find looking back at us the Face we implicitly long for and already know. It is set in another world, another light: yet it is here. As we realize this, our prayer widens until it embraces the extremes of awestruck adoration and confident love, and fuses them in one.

THE STIRRING OF THE PERFECT

Only Love, Charity, in its deep peacefulness and abiding joy, can embrace all human inconsistency and imperfection and see within it the stirring of the Perfect. But so God loves the world. Not its more spiritual inhabitants. Not its churchwardens and sacristans and pious old ladies—but the world.

ENWRAPPED IN LOVE

Everything, says Julian (of Norwich) in effect, whether gracious, terrible or malignant, is enwrapped in love: and is part of a world produced, not by mechanical necessity, but by passionate desire. Therefore nothing can really be mean, nothing despicable; nothing, however perverted, irredeemable. The blasphemous other-worldliness of the false mystic who conceives of matter as an evil thing and flies from its 'deceits,' is corrected by this loving sight. Hence, the more beautiful and noble a thing appears to us, the more we love it: for then we perceive within it the Divine ardour surging up towards expression, and share that simplicity and purity of vision in which most saints and some poets see all things 'as they are in God.'

This love-driven world of duration—this work within which the Divine Artist passionately and patiently expresses His infinite dream under finite forms—is held in another, mightier embrace. It is 'kept' says Julian. Paradoxically, the perpetual changeful energies of love and creation which inspire it, are gathered up and made complete within the unchanging fact of Being: the Eternal and Absolute, within which the world of things is set, as the tree is set in the supporting earth, the enfolding air. There, finally, is the rock and refuge of the seeking consciousness wearied by the ceaseless process of flux. There that flux exists in its wholeness 'all at once'; in a manner which we can never comprehend, but which in hours of withdrawal we may sometimes taste and feel. It is in man's moments of contact with this, when he penetrates beyond all images, however lovely, however significant, to that ineffable awareness which the mystics call 'Naked Contemplation'—since it is stripped of all the clothing with which reason and imagination drape and disguise both our devils and our gods—that the hunger and thirst of the heart is satisfied, and we receive indeed an assurance of ultimate Reality. This assurance is not the cool conclusion of a successful argument. It is rather the seizing at last of Something which we have ever felt near us and enticing us: the unspeakably simple because completely inclusive solution of all the puzzles of life.

OVERRULING LOVE

Though the soul may not seek God for any utilitarian reason, yet . . . because of her entire dependence on the unseen, she can ask with the assurance of a child for personal guidance and rescue; for the intimate concern of the Transcendent with her small and struggling life. Her faith, hope and love converge to produce this state of abandoned trust.

The action of that overruling love fails not. It is we that resist, ignore, are lost and bewildered because we do not abandon ourselves to the steady guiding power; become lost in multiplicity and forget the universals which condition our real life. Regret for the past, its errors and evil, and anxiety and bewilderment as regards the future, keep us enchained by succession, and our contact with the Abiding is lost. Nevertheless, as the life of prayer deepens it brings a gradual realization of the twofold character of all our experience; each event truly a part of this unceasing storm of succession, and yet each event directly linked with the quiet action of God. Through all the vicissitudes of trial, sin and conflict, the ground of the soul is rooted in His life; that country from which we are exiled, yet which is our home. . . . The ultimate humble trust of the little creature which first dared to say Abba! Father! is placed in the Absolute Love; and finds in the simple return to God the

Unchanging, that personal and permanent relation which is the ground of prayer, the sovereign remedy against temptation, and defence against the assaults of the world's ill.

DIVINE GIVE AND TAKE

Whoever will look at William Blake's great picture of the Creation of Adam, may gain some idea of the terrific yet infinitely compassionate character inherent in this concept of Divine Love: the agony, passion, beauty, sternness, and pity of the primal generating force. This love is eternally giving and taking—it is its very property, says Ruysbroeck, 'ever to give and ever to receive'—pouring its dower of energy into the soul, and drawing out from that soul new vitality, new love, new surrender. 'Hungry love,' 'generous love,' 'stormy love,' he calls it again and again. Streaming out from the heart of Reality, the impersonal aspect of the very Spirit of God, its creative touch evokes in man, once he becomes conscious of it, an answering storm of love. The whole of our human growth within the spiritual order is conditioned by the quality of this response, by the will, the industry, the courage, with which man accepts his part in the Divine give-and-take.

LOVE-AND-LOVELINESS

The Beautiful, says Hegel, is the spiritual making itself known sensuously. It represents, then, a direct message to us from the heart of Reality; ministers to us of more abundant life. Therefore the widening of our horizon which takes place when we turn in prayer to a greater world than that which the senses reveal to us, should bring with it a more poignant vision of loveliness, a more eager passion for Beauty as well as for Goodness and Truth.

When St. Augustine strove to express the intensity of his regret for wasted years, it was to his neglect of the Beauty of God that he went to show the poignancy of his feeling, the immensity of his loss. 'Oh Beauty so old and so new! too late have I loved thee!'

It needs a special training I think—a special and deliberate use of our faculties—if we are to avoid this deprivation; and learn as an integral part of our communion with Reality, to lay hold of the loveliness of the First and only Fair.

DIVINE BEAUTY

This should be the freely upspringing lyric beauty which is rooted in intense personal feeling; the living beauty of a living thing. Nor need we fear the reproach that here we confuse religion with poetry. Poetry ever goes like the royal banners before ascending life; therefore man may safely follow its leadership in his prayer, which is—or should be—life in its intensest form.

Consider the lilies; those perfect examples of a measured, harmonious, natural and creative life, under a form of utmost loveliness . . . It is the duty of all Christians to impart something of that flower-like beauty to their prayer; and only feeling of a special kind will do it—that humble yet passionate love of the beautiful which finds the perfect object of its adoration in God, and something of His fairness in all created things. St. Francis had it strongly, and certain other of the mystics had it too. In one of his rapturous meditations, Suso, for whom faith and poetry were—as they should be—fused in one, calls the Eternal Wisdom a 'sweet and beautiful wild flower.' He recognized that flowery charm which makes the Gospels fragrant and is included in the pattern which Christians are called to imitate if they can. Now if this quality is to be manifested in human life, it must first be sought and actualized . . . in prayer; because it is in the pure, sharp air of the spiritual order that it lives. It must spring up from within outwards, must be the reflection of the soul's communion with 'that Supreme Beauty which containeth in itself all goodness'; which was revealed to Angela of Foligno but which she 'could in no wise describe.' The intellect may and should conceive of this Absolute Beauty as well as it can; the will may—and must—be set on the attaining of it. But only by intuitive feeling can man hope to know it and only by love can he make it his own. The springs of the truest prayer and the deepest poetry—twin expressions of man's outward-going passion for that Eternity which is his home—rise very near together in the heart.

CREATOR AND CREATURE

What we have to find is a way of seeing the world which shall justify the saint, the artist and the scientist, and give each his full rights. Not a doctrine of watertight compartments, an opposition of appearance to reality. Rather, a doctrine of the indwelling of this visible world by an invisible yet truly existent world of spirit which, while infinitely transcending, yet everywhere supports and permeates the natural scene. Even to say this, is to blur the true issue by resort to the deceptive spatial language which colours and controls our thoughts and translate the dynamic and spiritual into static and intellectual terms.

The first demand we must make of such a diagram is that it shall at least safeguard, though it can never represent, all the best that man has learned to apprehend of the distinct and rich reality of God . . . For that which above all a genuine theism requires of our human ways of thinking, is the acknowledgement of two sorts or stages of reality, which can never be washed down into one: of a two-foldness that goes right through man's experience and cannot without impoverishment, be resolved. We may call these two sorts of reality, this two-foldness, by various names— Supernature and Nature, Eternity and Time, God and the world, Infinite and finite, Creator and creature. These terms do but emphasize one or another aspect of a total fact too great for us to grasp, without infringing the central truth of its mysterious duality: for God, as Plotinus says, 'never was the All. That would make Him dependent on His universe.'

II

CHRIST, THE EVIDENCE AND PROOF OF LOVE

IMMANENCE

I come in the little things,
Saith the Lord:
Not borne on morning wings
Of majesty, but I have set My Feet
Amidst the delicate and bladed wheat
That springs triumphant in the furrowed sod.
There do I dwell, in weakness and in power:
Not broken or divided, saith our God!
In your straight garden plot I come to flower:
About your porch My Vine
Meek, fruitful, doth entwine;
Waits, at the threshold, Love's appointed hour.

I come in the little things,
Saith the Lord:
Yea! on the glancing wings
Of eager birds, the softly pattering feet
Of furred and gentle beasts, I come to meet
Your hard and wayward heart. In brown bright eyes
That peep from out the brake, I stand confest.
On every nest
Where feathery Patience is content to brood
And leaves her pleasure for the high emprize
Of motherhood—
There doth My Godhead rest.

53

I come in the little things,
Saith the Lord:
My starry wings
I do forsake,
Love's highway of humility to take:
Meekly I fit My stature to your need.
In beggar's part
About your gates I shall not cease to plead—
As man, to speak with man—
Till by such art
I shall achieve My Immemorial Plan.
Pass the low lintel of the human heart.

For Christian experience the life and person of Christ stand apart as the greatest of self-revelations; the perfect self-expression of the Holy in human terms, and the supreme school and focus of man's adoring prayer. For here the invisible God, by the most wonderful of His condescensions, discloses His beauty and attraction—the brightness of His glory and the express image of His person—in a way that is mercifully adapted to our limitations and meets us on our own ground.

Therefore the events of Christ's life—alike the most strange and the most homely—are truly 'mysteries.' They contain far more than they reveal. They are charged with Spirit and convey the supernatural to those who are content to watch and adore. Because of this, Christian devotion moves to and fro between adoring and intimate prayer; passing through the incarnational veil to the Absolute Beauty shining through the incarnate veil. 'Let thy thoughts be always upward to God and direct thy prayer to Christ continually,' says Thomas à Kempis. Thus the great horizon gives its meaning to the welcoming figure; and the welcoming figure makes the great horizon safe and fair.

THE INFINITE LIFE

The events of Christ's life are well-named 'mysteries' for their meaning transcends the historical accidents and occasions which condition their outward form, and has an immortal relation with the interior life of men. There is a mounting revelation of the Spirit in and through this uttered Thought, the incarnate Word. The point of insertion has behind it the wealth and pressure of the Infinite Life.

THE HIGHWAY OF HUMILITY

The mystery of Reality enters history very gently by a human channel and shows the character of Perfect Love within the life of man; gives us something to hold on to, a Truth which is also a Way and a Life. What we see is not very sensational: but if we look at it steadily, it pierces the heart. First we see a baby and a long, hidden growth; and then the unmeasured outpouring and self-spending of an other-worldly love and mercy, teaching, healing, rescuing, transforming, but never trying to get anything for itself. And when we look deeper, we see beyond this a mysterious self-imparting and a more mysterious anguish and struggle; consummated at last in the most generous and lonely of deaths, issuing in a victory which has given life ever since to men's souls. Through this vivid life— what Christ does and how He does it, His prayer, His compassionate healing action, His use of suffering, His communion with God and man—the light of Reality floods our twilit inner lives; showing us the human transfigured by the Divine. This is what St. Ignatius Loyola intended and desired when he taught his pupils to 'contemplate the Mysteries of the Life of Christ.'

Few people do it properly. They are too anxious to get on and be practical: for the lesson of the one thing needful is a lesson which human nature instinctively resists. Yet we shall make our own small work of art all the better if we soak our souls in that beauty first.

HUMBLE SELF-ABANDONMENT

'God speaks in a Son' (as Hebrews has it), a Baby Son, and reverses all our pet values. He speaks in our language and shows us His secret beauty on our scale. We have got to begin, not by an arrogant other-worldliness, but by a humble recognition that human beings can be very holy, very full of God and that high-minded speculations about His nature need not be holy at all; that all life is engulfed in Him and He can reach out to us anywhere, at any level.

As the Christmas Day Gospel takes us back to the Mystery of the Divine Nature—*In the beginning was the Word*—so let us begin by thinking of what St. Catherine of Siena called the 'ocean Pacific of the Godhead' enveloping all life. The depth and richness of His being are entirely unknown to us, poor little scraps as we are! And yet the unlimited Life who is Love right through—who loves and is wholly present where He loves on every plane and at every point—so loved the world as to desire to give His essential thought, the deepest secrets of His heart, to this small, fugitive imperfect creation—to *us*. That seems immense.

And then the heavens open and what is disclosed? A Baby, God manifest in the flesh. The stable, the manger, the straw; poverty, cold, darkness—these form the setting for the Divine Gift. In this Child God gives His supreme message to the soul—Spirit to spirit—but in a human way. Outside in the fields the heavens open and the shepherds look up astonished to find the music and radiance of Reality all around them . . . We are not told that the Blessed Virgin Mary saw the Angels or heard the *Gloria* in the air. Her initiation had been quite different, like a quiet voice speaking in our deepest prayer: *The Lord is with thee!—Behold the handmaid of the Lord!* Humble self-abandonment is quite enough to give us God.

EMMANUEL

The world is not saved by evolution but by incarnation. The more deeply we enter into prayer the more certain we become of this. Nothing can redeem the lower and bring it back to health, but a life-giving incursion from the higher; a manifestation of the already present Reality. 'I came forth from the Father and am come into the world': and this perpetual advent—the response of the eternal Agape to Eros in his need—is the true coming into time of the Kingdom of Heaven. The Pentecostal energy and splendour is present to glorify every living thing: and sometimes our love reaches the level at which it sees this as a present fact and the actual is transfigured by the real.

What we look for, then, is not Utopia, but something which is given from beyond: Emmanuel, God with us, the whole creation won from rebellion and consecrated to the creative purposes of Christ. This means something far more drastic than the triumph of international justice and good social conditions. It means the transfiguration of the natural order by the supernatural: by the Eternal Charity. Though we achieve social justice, liberty, peace itself, though we give our bodies to be burned for these admirable causes, if we lack charity we are nothing. For the Kingdom is the Holy, not the moral; the Beautiful not the correct; the Perfect not the adequate; Charity not law.

THE MYSTERY OF LIFE

Look at the story of the Magi: those scholars of the ancient world, turning from their abstruse calculations and searching of the heavens because they saw a new star, and are driven to seek along fresh paths for a clue to the mystery of life. What they found does not seem at first sight what we should now call 'intellectually satisfying.' It was not a revelation of the Cosmic Mind but a poor little family party; yet there they were brought to their knees— because, like the truly wise, they were really humble-minded—before a little living, growing thing. The utmost man can achieve on his own here capitulates before the unspeakable and mysterious simplicity of the method of God; His stooping down to us, His self-disclosure at the very heart of life. After all the shepherds got there long before the Magi; and even so, the animals were already in position when the shepherds arrived. He comes to His own; the God of our natural life makes of that natural life the very material of His self-revelation. His smile kindles the whole universe; His hallowing touch lies upon all life. The animal world and the natural world have their own rights and their own place within the Thought of God. There never was a religion more deeply in touch with natural things than Christianity, although it is infinite in its scope.

DYNAMIC LOVE

If we consider Christ's own action, as He moves, a man amongst men, declaring the Kingdom of God, we see that He sets about this in the most practical way; not merely inviting men to think of the Transcendent, but bringing down into the texture of their lives the redeeming action of the Transcendent. He is singularly uninterested in lofty ideas and large projects, but greatly interested in redemptive acts. 'Jesus,' says St. Matthew, 'went about in all Galilee, preaching the good news of the Kingdom and healing all manner of disease and all manner of sickness among the people.' He was acting as a link between the outpouring love and harmony of the Life of God and the jangled and defective life of men. 'Tell John the blind see, the lame walk, the lepers are cleansed.' Human life is re-adjusted and made whole by the healing action of dynamic love, exercised by One whose life is identical with His prayer. His injunctions to His agents follow the same lines. They are to heal disharmony and misery wherever they find it; meeting with an eager and compassionate love the most repulsive aspects of life, touching the leper, ministering to the neurotic, seeking the degraded and lost.

Christ announced the one and only purpose of His ministry to be the bringing in of the Kingdom of God; by the quiet action of a flawless love giving back to our lost tormented planet its place in the orchestra of heaven.

CHRIST THE RESCUER

God enters human life not only to help, teach and complete it, but to overrule, transform, rescue and control circumstance—a saving energy intervening with an entire and noble freedom, constrained only by love. *Kyrie Eleison! Christe Eleison!* Lord have mercy! Christ have mercy!

It was like that when He went up to the disciples in the ship 'and the wind ceased ... and there was a calm.' Then the situation was transformed by His presence. One way or another, life brings every awakening Christian soul this experience. When we recognize and reflect on it—for it may come in a way that seems very simple—it fills us with awe and grateful love. God in Christ intervenes between us and the storm that threatens to overwhelm us. His power is brought into action just where our action fails; He comes to the rescue of those caught in the toils of circumstance. . . .

Sometimes it is on our soul that He lays His tranquillizing touch and stills the storm; sometimes on the hurly-burly of our emotional life, sometimes on events that we think must destroy us or the people and causes we love . . . We do feel sometimes as if we are left to ourselves to struggle with it all. He is away praying on the mountain, or He is asleep in the boat; the waves seem to be getting decidedly higher, the night is very dark . . . we begin to lose our nerve for life and no one seems to mind. Certainly life is not made soft for Christians; but it *is*, in the last resort, safe. The universe is safe for souls. The disciples were frightened, exhausted, soaked to the skin, but *not* destroyed. At the critical moment He went up into the ship and restored safety, sanity, peace. . . .

So Christ stands over against history and in its darkest and most dangerous moments we receive a new revelation of His power.

CHRIST THE TEACHER

Psychology of religion cannot teach us prayer, and ethics cannot teach us love. Only Christ can do that, and He teaches by the direct method, in and among the circumstances of life. He does not mind about our being comfortable. He wants us to be strong, able to tackle life and be Christians, be apostles in life, so we must be trained by the ups and downs, the rough and tumble of life. Team games are compulsory in the school of Divine Love; there must be no getting into a corner with a nice spiritual book.

When we consider the immense demands made on us: on our courage, initiative, patience, compassion, by the natural life we live here (if we take it as we should) what will be the demands, tensions, mighty opportunities of love and service offered to the mature soul by the life of the Eternal World? We are being educated by Christ, the Teacher for that world as well as this. You don't think Heaven will be soft chairs and Vi-springs do you? Christ the Teacher trains us for Heaven, the Kingdom of God, and links the Kingdom of God with the most homely and practical tests and duties and experiences; He never leaves them out. . . .

The clue to life He offers is not a bit of soft ribbon but a hard rope that will bear our weight but will also chafe our hands!

THE ORDINARY AND THE SUBLIME

This genius for the ordinary—this sacramental trans-figuring use of common life—which colours all the words and deeds of Jesus, was so deeply stamped upon the memories of His followers that it has triumphed over all their natural instinct for the impressive and abnormal; and has given to us, not a Hierophant of the Mysteries, but a patient Sower of the seed, a Shepherd, Healer, Comrade, loved and loving Master; a Maker of yokes on which the feeble staggering human creature can carry the balanced burden of physical and spiritual existence.

We are parochial little creatures: God must meet us in our parish if He is ever to meet us at all. If we are told to 'behold His glory,' know and love Him, He must somehow enter with His imperishable loveliness, the short life-circle of ordinary men. We cannot escape our own limitations and go to Him beyond the Spheres . . .

Where Plato declared 'the true order of going' to be a mounting up by means of the beauties of earth, step by step towards the unearthly and celestial Beauty; the Christian

Church—strong in her possession of the Divine paradox—compels her children to take the opposite route. She declares the true movement of the religious consciousness to be inwards, not outwards. It moves from the abstract and adoring sense of God Transcendent to the homely discovery of His revelation right down in history, in humblest surroundings and most simple concrete ways: bringing the adoring soul from the utmost confines of thought—*la forma universa di questa nodo*—to kneel before a poor person's baby born under the most unfortunate circumstances.

The figure of Christ stands so exactly on the confines between divine and human—so fully radiating God, while remaining so completely man 'of a reasonable soul and human flesh subsisting'—that men have never been able to decide in which category to place Him. Meditation seems more and more to show us the relation of history and eternity, our natural and supernatural environment, brought to a point in His person. The serial changes of man and the steadfast abidingness of God seem to co-exist in Him; and every act and word of His earthly life has, like His parables, a double reference. It shows us the perfect living-out of the life of nature, so that men have been quite satisfied to find in Him the supreme ethical teacher and model of human relationships; yet in and with this the achievement of something utterly beyond Nature—that state of soul and consequent transfiguration of existence, which He calls the Kingdom of God, and into which He brings His saints. . . .

Christ more perfectly discloses His Divine character by sitting at meals with sinners—being so wide, genial, strong and pure that He can take all human acts within His span—than by pursuing the traditional methods of ascetic saintliness.

JESUS, FULLY HUMAN AND FULLY DIVINE

Studying the earliest biographers and interpreters of Jesus, we find that it was neither His moral transcendence nor His special doctrine that struck them most. It was rather the growing certitude that something was here genuinely present in and with humanity, which was yet 'other' than humanity. From the beginning, the Christian claim that Christ is 'fully human and fully Divine' meant and means the effort to formulate the deeply-felt conviction that His person and life do not simply manifest the fullest possibilities of human nature evolving from within. In Him, we feel, we see beyond the world—'Jesus from the ground suspires' does not express all that the Incarnation means for us.

THE BRIDGE BETWEEN GOD AND MAN

When human thought, warmed by human love, first got to work on the facts which were found to transfigure human life wherever received; the forced conclusion of the matter was, that here something other than the development of history was involved. Here, by all sensitive spirits, the moulding of the Transcendent is vividly experienced; the Supernatural reaches man and man's world as never before, along the path of human personality. And if this be the true way of seeing things, then in the bold language of St. Catherine of Siena, philosophy itself can afford to regard the person of Jesus as a 'Bridge' between God and man, whereby 'the earth of humanity is joined to the greatness of the Deity.'

THE HOLY SPIRIT, THE AGENT OF LOVE

NIGHT ON THE MOUNTAIN

I

Night on the mountain. Soon I may not see
The sharp and spreading map,
The chequer-world of man's hard husbandry.
Comes white as wool the cloud veil that shall cap
The peak whereon I stand and stretch to thee.

Night on the mountain. Soft and silently
Out from their little dens the furred things creep:
They will not sleep
With valley-dwelling man, but wake to thee.
The fox from out its hole, the night bird from its nest,
I with the rest,
Yet not from any dear and hearted home
But from long exile come.

Long exile in the puzzling world, when all
Thy veils were close and bright
And picture set; yea, as a storied pall
Concealed thy night.
Long pilgrimage within the twisting lanes,
The deep and scented lanes, that wandered slow
Athwart the sleek profusion of the plains
But dared not seek
The solitary peak
To which thy lovers go.

Now the old words that once were mine and thine
Come to the lips and echo in the ear,
Now the white cloud draws near
And stills the restless limbs and shuts the peering sight
From all thing save thy night—
The caverned door of our unshuttered shrine.

II

Strange, holy night, Eternity's caress,
Most apt for happy lovers to enjoy;
Thou dost redeem the foolish dreams of men
Bewildered by the dreadful day's employ.
How the white flowers upon thy breast do burn
And tell thy dark excesses. Thou dost turn
Each candid primrose to a moon of light;
Thou dost enchant the fingers of the fern
Stretched from the woodland to assoil our sight
From the sharp day's distress.
When homely shapes put on a priestly dress,
When from the dewy fields new presences arise
And grave trees standing there
Lift up great arms in prayer;

When the dim ground
Hath soft mysterious movements of desire
And every hill converses with the skies;
'Tis then
Our little star at home in heaven is found,
And we and it are gathered to thy heart.
Then muted adoration hath its part,
Then comes the hush of grace and wraps us round,
Then comes the flame of love and gives us of its fire.

Then, undistracted by the heady sun,
We are with thee as once ere all began,
Made partners with the ardent worlds that run
Across thy bosom's span;
Knowing themselves to be
Radiant of love and light because they rest in thee.

Dear night, I love thee. Take me by the hand,
Make thou the ferment of my thought to cease.
Teach me thy wisdom. Let me understand
Thine unstruck music. Give my soul release
From the day's glare and din.
Lift thou the latch, that I may push the gate
And let my Darling in.
He stands without, he wearies not to wait
Before my threshold till
Thou hast made all things proper to our state
And every voice is still.
Then thou and he shall enter side by side,
Thy banner shall be set above his bride,
The curtains of thy splendour shall be spread
About our marriage bed.

THE INVASION OF ANOTHER ORDER

THERE is constantly implied in the religious outlook of the Old and New Testament writers, the expected invasion of another order over against the historical and human. Here, Spirit always represents the unconditioned action, the awful intervention of the very Life of God; at once a living spring and a devouring fire. The world of the Bible is not wholly built up by the quiet action of aqueous deposits. Its various structure witnesses to volcanic periods; when another order intervenes with power to compel and transform.

DIVINE VITALITY IMMANENT IN THE UNIVERSE

This same 'light wherein we see God' also shows to the enlightened mind the veritable character of the Holy Spirit; the Incomprehensible Love and Generosity of the Divine Nature, which emanates in an eternal procession from the mutual contemplation of Father and Son, 'for these two Persons are always hungry for love.' The Holy Spirit is the source of the Divine vitality immanent in the universe. It is an outflowing torrent of Good which streams through all heavenly spirits; it is a Flame of Fire that consumes all in the One; it is also the spark of transcendence latent in man's soul. The Spirit is the personal, Grace the impersonal, side of that energetic Love which enfolds and penetrates all life.

LORD AND LIFE-GIVER

'We have all been made to drink of one Spirit,' says St. Paul, as if this ineffable truth were a commonplace of religious experience. And this Spirit, says the Creed, is both Lord and Life-giver; the Absolute God acting and bringing the whole Trinity into the soul which thus becomes the Temple of the Holy Giver of Life.

THE HOLY SPIRIT: DOWER AND POWER

The last message of Evelyn Underhill

From the very beginning the Church has been sure that the series of events which were worked out to their inevitable end in Holy Week sum up and express the deepest secrets of the relation of God to men. That means, of course, that Christianity can never be merely a pleasant or consoling religion. It is a stern business. It is concerned with the salvation through sacrifice and love of a world in which, as we can all see now, evil and cruelty are rampant. Its supreme symbol is the Crucifix—the total and loving self-giving of man to the redeeming purposes of God.

Because we are all the children of God we all have our part to play in His redemptive plan; and the Church consists of those loving souls who have accepted this obligation, with all it costs. Its members are all required to live, each in their own way, through the sufferings and self-abandonment of the Cross; as the only real contribution which they can make to the redemption of the world. Christians, like their Master, must be ready to accept the worst that evil and cruelty can do to them, and vanquish it by the power of love.

For if sacrifice, total self-giving to God's mysterious purpose, is what is asked of us, His answer to that sacrifice is the gift of power. Easter and Whitsuntide complete the Christian Mystery by showing us first our Lord Himself and then His chosen apostles possessed of a new power—

the power of the Spirit—which changed every situation in which they were placed. That supernatural power is still the inheritance of every Christian, and our idea of Christianity is distorted and incomplete unless we rely on it. It is this power and only this which can bring in the new Christian society of which we hear so much. We ought to pray for it; expect it, trust it; and as we do this, we shall gradually become more and more sure of it.[1]

THE ENERGY OF LOVE

The energy of love will never do for us that which we ought to do for ourselves; but will ever back up the creature's efforts by its grace, coming into action just where our action fails. This is a secret that has always been known to men and women of prayer; something we can trust and that acts in proportion to our trust. Sometimes it is on our soul that the tranquillizing touch is laid: sometimes the hurly-burly of our emotional life, which threatens to overwhelm us, is mysteriously stilled. Sometimes events, which we think must destroy us or those whom we love, are strangely modified by the Spirit that indwells and rules them. More and more as we go on with the Christian life we learn the absolute power of Spirit over circumstance. God in His richness and freedom coming as a factor into every situation; overruling the stream of events which make up our earthly existence and through these events moulding our souls, quickening and modifying our lives at every point. . . . 'The power of God present unto salvation,' says St. Paul (not the power of God present unto comfort); this is the very essence of the Gospel. We are

[1] This was the last letter Evelyn Underhill wrote to a Prayer Group she led, for Easter, 1941. She died two months later on *Corpus Christi*.

held and penetrated by a personal Spirit, a never-ceasing Presence, that intervenes to use or overrule events. The more freely, simply and humbly the soul is abandoned to this penetrating and encompassing power, the more it becomes conscious—dimly yet surely—of its constant, stern, yet loving action through all the circumstances of life. To resist that action means conflict and suffering. To accept it may still mean suffering; but a suffering that is sweetened by love.

MUTUAL QUEST: GOD'S AND MAN'S

If we ask as a summing-up of the whole matter: *Why* man is thus to seek the Eternal, through, behind and within the ever-fleeting—the answer is that he cannot . . . help doing it sooner or later: for his heart is never at rest till it finds itself there. But he often wastes a great deal of time before he realizes this. And perhaps we may find the reason why man—each man—is thus pressed towards some measure of union with Reality, in the fact that his conscious will, thus and thus only, becomes an agent of the veritable purposes of life: of that Power which in and through mankind, conserves and slowly presses towards realization the noblest aspirations of each soul. This power and push we may call if we like in the language of realism, the tendency of our space-time universe towards deity; or, in the language of religion, the working of the Holy Spirit. And since, so far as we know, it is only in man that life becomes self-conscious, and ever more and more self-conscious, with the deepening and widening of his love and his thought; so it is only in man that it can dedicate the will and desire which are life's central qualities, to the furtherance of this Divine creative aim.

CO-OPERATION WITH THE SPIRIT

This simplifying and supernaturalizing of the whole drive and intention of our life, by its immersion in the great movement of the Infinite Life, is itself the work of the Creative Spirit. It is only possible because that Spirit already indwells the soul's ground, and there pursues the secret alchemy of love; more and more possessing and transmuting us with every small movement of acceptance or renunciation in which we yield ourselves to the quiet action of God. It is true that the soul hardly perceives the separate moments of this mysterious action; and only by a view which takes in long stretches of experience, can realize the changes which it works.

Yet our own self-discipline and suffering, our willing acquiescence and adjustment to circumstances, could do little here, did they not work together with the inciting, moulding, indwelling Power; submitting us to that secret and passive purification which cleanses will and emotion of unreal attachments, and perfectly unites the poor little love and will of man with the universal Love and Will of God. Then when the whole movement of our being is freely given in love to the purposes of Spirit, and takes its small place in the eternal order, we find our place and our peace. We learn to give significance and worth to our homeliest duties by linking all the chain-like activities of daily life with His overruling and unchanging Reality: 'that most inspiring and darling relation,' says von Hügel, wherein 'you have each single act, each single moment, joined directly to God—Himself not a chain, but one great Simultaneity.'

CREATIVE ACTIVITY OF THE SPIRIT

The Coming of the Kingdom is perpetual. Again and again freshness, novelty, power from beyond the world, break in by unexpected paths, bringing unexpected change.

Those who cling to tradition and fear all novelty in God's relation with His world, deny the creative activity of the Holy Spirit, and forget that what is now tradition was once innovation: that the real Christian is always a revolutionary, belongs to a new race and has been given a new name and a new song. God is with the future. The supernatural virtue of Hope blesses and supports every experiment made for the glory of His Name and the good of souls: and even when violence and horror seem to over-whelm us, discerns the secret movement of the Spirit inciting to sacrifice and preparing new triumphs for the Will. In the Church, too, this process of renovation from within, this fresh invasion of Reality must constantly be repeated if she is to escape the ever-present danger of stagnation. She is not a static institution but the living Body of the living Christ—the nucleus of the Kingdom, in this world. Thus loyalty to her supernatural calling will mean flexibility to its pressures and demands and also a constant adjustment to that changing world to which she brings the unchanging gifts. But only in so far as her life is based on prayer and self-offering will she distinguish rightly between these implicits of her vocation and the suggestions of im-patience or self-will.

Yet the coming of the Kingdom does not necessarily mean the triumph of this visible Church; nor of that which is sometimes called the Christian Social Order. It means something far more deep, subtle and costly: the reign of God, the all-demanding and all-loving in individual hearts, overruling all the adverse powers which dominate

human life—the vigorous survivals from our animal past
which are nourished by our egotism and support its im-
plicit rebellion against God—fear and anger, greed and
self-assertion, jealousy, impatience and discontent.   It
means the re-ordering, the quieting, the perfecting of our
turbulent interior life, the conquest of our rampant indi-
vidualism by God's supernatural action; and that same
supernatural action gradually making each human life
what it is meant to be—a living part of the Body of Christ,
a sacramental disclosure of the Splendour of God.

THE SEVEN GIFTS OF THE SPIRIT

Spiritual writers tell us to expect certain qualities which
are traditionally called 'the seven gifts of the spirit'; and
if we study the special nature of these gifts we see that they
are the names of linked characters or powers which work
together an enhancement and clarification of the whole
personality—a tuning-up of human nature to fresh levels,
a sublimation of its primitive instincts. The first pair of
qualities which are to mark our spiritual humanity are
called Godliness and Fear. By these are meant that solemn
sense of direct relationship with an eternal order, that
gravity and awe which we ought to feel in the presence of
the mysteries of the universe; the fear of the Lord which is
the beginning of wisdom. From these grow the gifts called
Knowledge, that is the power of discerning true from false
values, of choosing a good path through the tangled world,
and Strength, the steady central control of the diverse
forces of the self: perhaps the gift most needed by our
distracted generation. 'Through the gift of spiritual
strength,' says Ruysbroeck, 'a man transcends all creaturely
things and possesses himself, powerful and free.' This is

surely a power which we should desire for the children of the future and get for them if we can.

We see that the first four gifts of the spirit will govern the adjustment of man to his earthly life: that they will immensely increase the value of his personality in the social order, will clarify his mind and judgement, confer nobility on his aims. The last three gifts—those called Counsel, Understanding and Wisdom—will govern his intercourse with the spiritual order. By Counsel, the spiritual writers mean that inward voice which, as the soul matures, urges us to leave the transitory, and seek the eternal: and this not as an act of duty, but as an act of love. When that voice is obeyed, the result is a new spiritual Understanding; which, says Ruysbroeck again, may be 'likened to the sunshine, which fills the air with a simple brightness, and lights all forms and shows the distinctions of all colours.' Even so does this spiritual gift irradiate the whole world with a new splendour, and shows us secrets that we never guessed before. Poets know flashes of it, and from it their power proceeds; for it enables its possessor to behold life truly, that is, from the angle of God, not from the angle of man.

III

CHURCH AND SACRAMENTS

THE CHURCH, THE HOME OF LOVE

MISSA CANTATA

Once in an Abbey-church, the whiles we prayed
  All silent at the lifting of the Host,
A little bird through some high window strayed;
      And to and fro
      Like a wee angel lost
That on a sudden finds its heaven below,
      It went the morning long,
And made our Eucharist more glad with song.

It sang, it sang! and as the quiet priest
  Far off about the lighted altar moved
The awful substance of that mystic feast
      All hushed before,
      It, like a thing that loved
Yet loved in liberty, would plunge and soar
      Beneath the vault in play
And thence toss down the oblation of its lay.

The walls that went our sanctuary around
  Did, as of old, to that sweet summons yield.
New scents and sounds within our gates were found;
      The cry of kine,
      The fragrance of the field,
All woodland whispers, hastened to the shrine:
      The country-side was come
Eager and joyful, to its spirit's home.

Far-stretched I saw the cornfield and the plough,
    The scudding cloud, the cleanly-running brook,
The humble, kindly turf, the tossing bough
              That all their light
              From Love's own furnace took—
This altar, where one angel brownly bright
              Proclaimed the sylvan creed,
And sang the Benedictus of the mead.

All earth was lifted to communion then,
    All lovely life was there to meet its King;
Ah, not the little arid souls of men
              But sun and wind
              And all desirous thing
The ground of their beseeching here did find;
    All with one self-same bread,
And all by one eternal priest, were fed.

When the Christian looks at the Crucifix, he looks at that which is for him the Pattern of all perfection; the double revelation of God's love towards man and man's love towards God, the heart of Charity. But he is also looking at the Church, that real Church which is a holy and living Sacrifice eternally self-offered to God; the Body of Christ, the number of whose members no man knows but God alone, and which is the living instrument of His creative love within this world. 'Wherever Christ is,' said St. Ignatius of Antioch, 'there is the Catholic Church.' So, to be a member of the Church means not merely conformity to an institution, but incorporation in that living organism which only exists to express the Thought of God. It means becoming part of that perpetual sacrifice which continues in space and time the life of Incarnate Charity. In the name of all her members the Church comes up to the altar with awe and thanksgiving, and there, on the very frontiers of the unseen world, she gives herself that she may receive the Food of Eternal Life. So the inner life of each one of those members must have in it the colour of sacrifice, the energy of a redeeming love, if it is to form part of the living Soul of the Church. The unceasing liturgic life of the official Church, her prayer and adoration, her oblation and communion, only has meaning as the expression of that soul: the voice of the Communion of Saints. But as this, it has a meaning, a splendour and claim on us, far transcending those private prayers to which we are apt to give priority. The whole poetry of man's relation to the unseen Love is hidden in the Liturgy: with its roots in history, its eyes set upon Eternity, its mingled outbursts of praise and supplication, penitence and delight, it encloses and carries forward the devotion of the individual soul, lost in that mighty melody.

THE CHURCH'S FELLOWSHIP OF LOVE

The reality of the Church does not abide in us; it is not a spiritual Rotary Club. Its reality abides in the One God, the ever-living One Whose triune Spirit fills it by filling each one of its members. We build up the Church best, not by a mere overhaul of the fabric and furniture, desirable as this may sometimes be, but by opening ourselves more and more with an entire and humble generosity to that Spirit— God—Who is among us as one that serveth and reaches out through His Church towards the souls of men. Thus the real life of that Church consists in the mutual love and dependence, the common prayer, adoration and self-offering of the whole inter-penetrating family of spirits who have dared to open their souls without condition to that all-demanding, all-giving Spirit of Charity, in Whom we live and move and without Whom we should not exist.

INSTITUTIONAL RELIGION

To join in simplicity and without criticism in the common worship, humbly receiving its good influences, is one thing. This is like the drill of the loyal soldier; welding him to his neighbours, giving him the corporate spirit and forming in him the habits he needs. But to stop short at that drill and tell the individual that drill is the essence of his life and all his duty, is another thing altogether. It confuses means and end; destroys the balance between liberty and law. If the religious institution is to do its real

work in furthering the life of the Spirit, it must introduce
a more rich variety into its methods; and thus educate
souls of every type not only to be members of the group
but also to grow up to the full richness of the personal life.
It must offer them—as indeed Catholicism does to some
extent already, both easy emotion and difficult mystery;
both dramatic ceremony and ceremonial silence. It must
also give them all its hoarded knowledge of the inner life
of prayer and contemplation, of the remaking of the moral
nature on supernatural levels: all the gold that there is in
the deposit of faith. And it must not be afraid to impart
that knowledge in modern terms which all can understand. All this it can and will do if its members sufficiently
desire it: which means, if those who care intensely for the
life of the Spirit accept their corporate responsibilities.
In the last resort, criticism of the Church, of Christian
institutionalism, is really criticism of ourselves. Were we
more spiritually alive, our spiritual homes would be the
real nesting places of new life. That which the Church is
to us is the result of all that we bring to, and ask from,
history: the impact of our present and its past.

THE CHURCH'S WORSHIP

Christian worship in its wholeness must include or imply
such equal, loving and costly responses to the threefold
Reality as we find, for example, in the writings of St. Paul
(*Rom.* xi. 33–36; I *Cor.* ii. 6–16, etc.): awestruck adoration
of the self-existent Eternal, 'the only Wise God,' total self-
offering to Him in Christ, and an active and grateful
recognition of the Holy Spirit of God, in His creative
guiding and purifying action upon the Church and the soul.
It involves then, an adoring acknowledgement: first of God's
cosmic splendour and otherness, next of His redemptive

and transfiguring action revealed in history, and last of His immanent guidance of life. . . . Christian worship is never a solitary undertaking. Both on its visible and invisible sides, it has a thoroughly social and organic character. The worshipper, however lonely in appearance, comes before God as a member of a great family; part of the Communion of Saints, living and dead. His own small effort of adoration is offered 'in and for all.' The first words of the Lord's Prayer are always there to remind him of his corporate status and responsibility in its double aspect. On one hand, he shares the great life and action of the Church, the Divine Society; however he may define that difficult term, or wherever he conceives its frontiers to be drawn. He is immersed in that life, nourished by its traditions, taught, humbled and upheld by its saints. His personal life of worship, unable for long to maintain itself alone, has behind it two thousand years of spiritual culture, and around it the self-offering of all devoted souls. Further, his public worship and commonly his secret devotion too, are steeped in history and tradition; and apart from them cannot be understood. There are few things more remarkable in Christian history than the continuity through many vicissitudes and under many disguises of the dominant strands in Christian worship. On the other hand the whole value of this personal life of worship abides in the completeness with which it is purified from all taint of egotism, and the selflessness and simplicity with which it is added to the common store. Here the individual must lose his life to find it; the longing for personal expression, personal experience, safety, joy, must more and more be swallowed up in Charity. For the goal alike of Christian sanctification and Christian worship is the ceaseless self-offering of the Church, in and with Christ her Head, to the increase of the glory of God.

THE COMMUNION OF SAINTS

The invisible but most actual incorporation of all awakened souls in one Supernatural Society embracing life and death, past and present in its span: this is what Christianity means by the Communion of Saints. Of that vast Supernatural Society, with its countless types of soul and vocation,—active, intellectual, mystical, speculative, intercessory, sacrificial—co-operating for one great end, the visible Church is or should be a sacramental expression.

PRAYING WITH THE CHURCH

The whole poetry of man's unseen relation to the unseen Love is hidden in the Liturgy: with its roots in history, its eyes set upon Eternity, its mingled outbursts of praise and supplication, penitence and delight, it encloses and carries forward the devotion of the individual soul, lost in that mighty melody. To say, then, that we believe the corporate voice of those who make this melody, whose separate lives are lost in it and who are our companions in the Way, begins to look like common sense. We are units in their mighty procession, and they can teach us how to walk.

THE WHOLE BODY

In work and prayer, suffering and self-conquest, we are never to forget that we do not act alone or for ourselves. We act with and for the whole Body. The prayer of the individual Christian is always the prayer of the whole Church; therefore it is infinite in its scope.

BRACING SOCIETY

We all know what a help it is to live amongst and be intimate with, keen Christians; how much we owe in our lives to contact with them and how hard it is to struggle on alone in a preponderantly non-Christian atmosphere. In the saints we always have the bracing society of keen Christians. We are always in touch with the classic standard. Their personal influence still radiates, centuries after they have left the earth, reminding us of the infinite variety of ways in which the Spirit of God acts on men through men, and reminding us, too, of our own awful responsibility in this matter. The saints are the great experimental Christians, who, because of their unreserved self-dedication have made the great discoveries about God; and as we read their lives and works they will impart to us just so much of these discoveries as we are able to bear. Indeed, as we grow more and more, the saints tell us more and more: disclosing at each fresh reading secrets we did not suspect. Their books are the work of specialists from whom we can humbly learn more of God and our own souls.

II

THE SACRAMENTS, THE CHANNELS OF LOVE

CORPUS CHRISTI

I

Come, dear Heart!
The fields are white to harvest: come and see
As in a glass the timeless mystery
Of love, whereby we feed
On God, our bread indeed.
Torn by the sickles, see him share the smart
Of travailing Creation: maimed, despised,
Yet by his lovers the more dearly prized
Because for us he lays his beauty down—
Last toll paid by perfection for our loss!
Trace on these fields his everlasting Cross,
And o'er the stricken sheaves the Immortal Victim's crown.

II

From far horizons came a Voice that said,
'Lo! from the hand of Death take thou thy daily bread.'
Then I, awakening, saw
A splendour burning in the heart of things:
The flame of living love which lights the law
Of mystic death that works the mystic birth.
I knew the patient passion of the earth,
Maternal, everlasting, whence there springs
The Bread of Angels and the life of man.

III

Now in each blade
I, blind no longer, see
The glory of God's growth: know it to be
An earnest of the Immemorial Plan.
Yea, I have understood
How all things are one great oblation made:
He on our altars, we on the world's rood.
Even as this corn,
Earth-born,
We are snatched from the sod;
Reaped, ground to grist,
Crushed and tormented in the Mills of God,
And offered at Life's hands, a living Eucharist.

SACRAMENTAL GRACE

THE sacraments are a perpetual witness that man needs something done to him here and now. They declare that an access of Supernature will reach him most easily along natural paths. Their whole emphasis is on the given-ness. They remind us that our innate thirst for the Infinite is not the governing fact of our religious life and cannot be satisfied by any effort we are able to make. That Infinite must come to us before we can go to it; and it is within the sensory and historical frame of human experience that such super-natural gifts are best and most surely received by our successive and sense-conditioned souls. Thus the sacramental principle continues to press upon us that profound truth which the Incarnation so vividly exhibits: that the whole of man's spiritual history, both corporate and solitary, involves and entirely rests in the free self-giving of God—is conditioned from first to last by the action of His all-penetrating, prevenient and eternal love. . . . Through the Christian sacraments that self-giving, of which the Incarnation is the supreme example, finds another and a continuous expression: sense here becoming the vehicle through which the very Spirit of Life enters into the little lives of men.

THE NECESSITY OF SACRAMENTS

Sacramentalism emerging as a primary means of worship, appropriate to the nature and situation of man, grows and deepens with our growth. It has something to give the most naïve of primitives; its possibilities have never been exhausted by the most supernaturalized of saints. For it reveals God, the Supernatural, ever at work seeking and finding us through the natural; the objects and actions of our temporal experience as the effective means of our deepest and most transforming apprehensions of Eternity, and our most insistent invitations to worship coming to us where we are, and taking us as we are—creatures of soul and body, conditioned by time and space. Therefore the cultus which excludes sacraments does not in consequence draw nearer to God; but renounces a sovereign means by which He is self-imparted to us, and in and through which His action may be recognized and adored. It is true that sacramental methods are always open to the dangers of formalism and exteriorization, and may even slide down into a crass materialism. Yet, on the other hand, it is those who have reached out through the sensible to an apprehension of the supra-sensible, who realize most fully the deep mystery and unexhausted possibilities which abide in the world of sense, and therefore its power of conveying to us that which lies beyond, and gives to it significance and worth.

VEHICLES OF THE ETERNAL CHARITY

The fully Christian life is a Eucharistic life: that is, a natural life conformed to the pattern of Jesus, given in its wholeness to God, laid on His altar as a sacrifice of love, and consequently transformed by His inpouring life, to be used to give life and food to other souls. It will be according to its measure and special call, adoring, declaratory, intercessory and redemptive: but always a vehicle of the Supernatural. The creative spirit of God is a redemptive and cherishing love; and it is as friends and fellow-workers with the Spirit, tools of the Divine redemptive action, that Christians are required to live. 'You are the body of Christ,' said St. Augustine to his communicants. That is to

say, in you and through you the method and work of the
Incarnation must go forward. You are meant to incarnate
in your lives the theme of your adoration. You are to be
taken, consecrated, broken and made means of grace;
vehicles of the Eternal Charity.

Thus every Christian communicant volunteers for translation into the supernatural order, and is self-offered for the
supernatural purposes of God. The Liturgy leads us out
towards Eternity, by way of the acts in which men express
their need of God and relation to God. It commits every
worshipper to the adventure of holiness, and has no meaning
apart from this.

THE ABIDING AND THE EVANESCENT

Though the degree in which each type of soul will
receive its spiritual food thus mixed with sense-elements,
will vary greatly, yet there must plainly be some such
physical reference in every healthy spiritual life. The fact
that such a life seeks in its measure to incarnate, and give
physical expression to the Eternal, makes this inevitable.
Reflecting on these facts, we are no longer amazed that
Christian initiation is accomplished by 'a little oil, a little
water, some fragments of bread and a chalice of wine' . . .

The symbol, the thing, through which men reached out
to and apprehended the Infinite, becomes the path by which
the present Infinite itself, with its fresh dower of life and
grace, comes into the little lives of men. As in great poetry
linked words are suffused with an unearthly glow and
splendour, and carry a heightened significance far beyond
their literal meaning: so in the sacraments, things and deeds
which emerge from the common stock of human experience
are suffused with a supernatural splendour and become
for the soul genuine 'vehicles of grace.'

DIVINE AND HUMAN CHARITY

Every Eucharist is a fresh act, a fresh declaration of love, freshly conditioned by the particular responses of the souls given to its movement: each of whom has an irreplaceable part to fill in the Church's total prayer. It is a new picture of the encounter of Divine and human charity; a work of art which always remains within the great tradition, yet bears its own witness to the impact of the Heavenly Beauty on each praying soul, with the variation occasioned by the individual and corporate response of these souls. But in every rite, though with many variations in temper, order, and emphasis we find the liturgic expression of certain fundamental truths about God and His relation to man. Thus all ancient liturgies begin by an invocation of the Holy Trinity; bringing to mind that mysterious Reality of the Divine Nature, lying far beyond our comprehension, which is yet the inciting cause, the object, and the theme of Eucharistic worship. But they pass quickly from that swift and awestruck contemplation of pure Being to the acknowledgement of man's insufficiency, dependence and faultiness, matched against the demands of the Holy, the splendour and perfection of God. Contrition succeeds vision; as always in any genuine experience of the Divine.

THE CHRISTIAN PARADOX

Without man's small offering (at the Eucharist) nothing would have been done. The loaves must be given, and at his own cost, before they can become the gathering-points of the supernatural care, blessed, broken, and distributed, and so the Bread of Life given to the soul. 'Why that's a bit of my own baking!' said the woman in the old story, when the Holy Food was put into her hand. True, there is no proportion between the little human offering and the divine gift. Yet even here where more than anywhere we feel our entire dependence and helplessness, will and grace rise and fall together, the double action between God and the soul is maintained. Incited by God, yet of its own free choice responding to that incitement, the fugitive and derivative creature draws near to the Unconditioned and Unchanging, and feeds directly on the Divine generosity; that, purified, transformed and strengthened, it may take up in its turn the vocation of charity and give itself without stint. Communion with Christ is communion with a life-giving Victim: and union with Christ is union with self-spending Love. The Church, the Bride of Christ, can only live in time the supernatural life, if there is a perpetual self-imparting to her and to all her members of this, the secret of all supernatural life.

CELESTIAL NOURISHMENT

The symbolism of food plays a large part in all religions, and especially in Christianity. As within the mysteries of the created order we must take food and give food—more, must take life and give life—we are already in touch with the 'life-giving and terrible mysteries of Christ'—Who indwells that order; for all is the sacramental expression of His all-demanding and all-giving Life. We accept our constant dependence on physical food as a natural and inevitable thing. Yet it is not necessarily so: there are creatures which are free from it for long periods of time. But perhaps because of his border-line status, his embryonic capacity for God, man is kept in constant memory of his own fragility, unable to maintain his existence for long without food from beyond himself; his bodily life dependent on the humble plants and animals that surround him, his soul's life on the unfailing nourishment of the life of God. 'I am the Bread of Life that came down from heaven. He that eateth of this bread shall live for ever.' Eternal Life is the gift, the self-imparting of the Eternal God. We cannot claim it in our own right.

THE LIVING CHRIST

The conviction of the intimate presence of a living Lord, which is still the real strength and common possession of Catholic and Evangelical doctrine, was the 'mystery of faith' which distinguished the first Christian assemblies. There seems little doubt that it was closely associated with the Eucharist, the capital importance of which is clear from the references in Acts and Corinthians. But at first the homely ceremony of the Breaking of the Bread—which had not yet become a standardized liturgical action—seems less to have been the occasion of the Presence, than an incident in the total act of thankful remembrance and adoring communion with the Risen Master; which transcended and included this ritual expression. The discourses of Jesus given in the fourteenth and fifteenth chapters of the Fourth Gospel restore to us the heart of that belief and practice by which the first Christian groups—or at least their most devoted members—lived, and in which they met suffering and persecution with joy. It is in their light that we shall best understand the worship of the Apostolic Church.

SELF-OBLATION

The Eucharist is first the Church's representation before God of the perfect self-offering of Christ; that threefold oblation of the Upper Room, Gethsemane and Calvary, in which all the deepest meanings of sacrifice are gathered and declared. Secondly, it is her own self-offering, and that of each of her members, in and with Christ her head: since His sacrifice 'once for all in fact externalized on Calvary, is ever real in the inward and heavenly sphere.'[1] To that inward and heavenly sphere the Church by her Eucharistic worship is admitted to join her sacrificial acts to the eternal self-offering of her Lord. These sacrificial acts, this total and loving dedication of life to the purposes of the Eternal—whether expressed in ritual action or not—form the very heart of her liturgic life. For the fullest act of worship, whether of Church or of the soul, must be the surrender of the created life to the purposes of the continuing Incarnation: a mergence of the created will in that single stream of Charity which manifests the Divine Will.

THE CONSUMMATION OF WORSHIP

The Christian hope of the future is that . . . the true message and meaning of the Incarnation will come to be more deeply understood: and the demand on man's worshipping love and total self-offering, will receive a more complete response—a response stretching upward in awe-struck contemplation to share that adoring vision of the Principle which is 'the inheritance of the saints in light,' and downwards and outwards in loving action, to embrace and so transform the whole world. When this happens, Christian sacramental worship will at last disclose its full meaning and enter into its full heritage. For it will be recognized as the ritual sign of our deepest relation with Reality, and so of the mysterious splendour of our situation

[1] Oliver Quick, *The Christian Sacraments*, p. 198.

and our call: the successive life of man freely offered in oblation, and the abiding life of God in Christ received, not for our own sakes, but in order to achieve that transfiguration of the whole created universe, that shining forth of the splendour of the Holy, in which the aim of worship shall be fulfilled.

IV

THE SPIRITUAL LIFE

LIFE, THE SCHOOL OF LOVE

THOUGHTS ABOUT HEAVEN

I

Heaven's not a place.
Where time doth race
Across the flatted fields of edgeless space
Thou shalt not hear its news, nor its retreat discover.
No! 'tis a dance
Where love perpetual,
Rhythmical,
Musical,
Maketh advance
Loved one to lover.

II

Heaven's not a rest.
No! but to battle with new zest:
Untired, with warrior joy
The sharp clean spirit to employ
On life's new enterprise.
It's the surprise
Of keen delighted mind
That wakes to find
Old fetters gone,
Strong shining immortality put on.

III

Heaven is to be
In God at last made free,
There more and more
Strange secrets of communion to explore:
Within the mighty movements of His will
Our tangled loves fulfil:
To pluck the rosemary we cannot reach
With the mind's span,
And so at last
Breathe the rich fragrance of our hoarded past
And learn the slow unfolding of the plan.
Together to unroll
The blazoned story of the pilgrim soul;
All the long ardent pain,
The craving and the bliss at last made plain.
Sometimes to sleep
Locked each to each
Within his deep,
Or playing in his wave
The sudden splendour of the flood to brave:
Great tide of his undimmed vitality
That breaks in beauty on the world's wide beach
And draws all life again toward its heart,
Stirring to new and mutual increase
Love-quickened souls therein that have their part,
Therein that find their peace.

'WHEN the evening of this life comes,' says St. John of the Cross, 'you will be judged on love.' The only question asked about the soul's use of its house and the gifts that were made to it will be: 'Have you loved well?' All else will be resumed in this; all thoughts, beliefs, desires, struggles and achievements, all complex activities . . . For Faith is nothing unless it be the obscure vision of a loved Reality; and Hope is nothing unless it be the confidence of perfect love. So, too, with all the persons, events, opportunities, conflicts and choices proposed for the soul's purification and growth. Was everything that was done, done for love's sake? Were all the doors opened that the warmth of Charity might fill the whole house; the windows cleaned that they might more and more radiate from within its mysterious divine light? Is the separate life of the house more and more merged in the mighty current of the city's life? Is it more and more adapted to the city's sacred purpose—the saving radiation of the Perfect within an imperfect world? For this is Charity; the immense expansion of personality effected by the love of God, weaving together the natural and the supernatural powers of the soul and filling them with its abundant life. Overflowing the barriers of preference, passing through all contrary appearance, it mediates the Divine pity and generosity to every mesh and corner of creation and rests at last in God, Who is the life and love of every soul.

THE CONSUMMATION OF LOVE

Through the Christian revelation men were shown, in a way that they could receive though never wholly understand, the nature of that Absolute Love which moves to their destiny all stars and all souls. And the term of that process is the Eternal Life, the perfect consummation which God has prepared for those that love Him; in other words, all who really want it. 'This is eternal life; to know Thee, the one true God,' and have our eyes opened on the Fact of facts, the soul's unique satisfaction, Whom to know is to adore. Christ in His great intercession asked only this for those He loved; this real life, poised in God. 'That they may be in us'; each tiny separate spirit absorbed in the mighty current of the Divine Charity. 'I in them and Thou in Me, that they may be perfected into one'; this is the consummation we look for, that share in the life of Reality which is prepared for men.

And further, the history of those souls whom that living God awakens, besets, and purifies by the action of His stern untiring love is unintelligible unless within that real life, all those faculties He is here bringing forth in them achieve the perfection which here they never reach. We are to expect the pure joy of a keen, unbaffled intelligence, of an unhindered vision of beauty; ears that can hear what the universe is always trying to say to us, hearts at last capable of a pure and unlimited love. Then that sense of reaching forward, of coming up to the verge of a world of unbounded realities, which haunts our best moments of prayer and communion, will be fulfilled. 'I look for the life of the world to come,' and see hints of it everywhere. . . .

Every human life, however humble, can do something to hasten or retard the triumph of the Eternal Charity. For God is not the God of the invisible creation alone. The new, the more real life that we expect must penetrate every level of existence and every relationship—politics, industry, science, art, our attitude to one another, our attitude to living nature—spiritualizing and unselfing all this; subduing it to the transforming action of 'the intellectual radiance, full of love.'

THE EMERGENCE OF LOVE

Here is our little planet, chiefly occupied, to our view, in rushing round the sun; but perhaps found from another angle to fill quite another part in the cosmic scheme. And on this apparently unimportant speck, wandering among systems of suns, the appearance of life and its slow development and ever-increasing sensitization; the emerging of pain and pleasure; and presently man with his growing capacity for self-affirmation and self-sacrifice, for rapture and for grief. Love with its unearthly happiness, unmeasured devotion, and limitless pain; all the ecstasy, all the anguish that we extract from the rhythm of life and death. It is much really for one little planet to bring to birth.

And presently another music, which some—not many perhaps yet in comparison with its population—are able to hear. The music of a more inward life, a sort of fugue in which the eternal and temporal are mingled; and here and there some already who respond to it. Those who hear it would not all agree that it is something different in kind from the rhythm of life and death. And in their surrender to this—to which, as they feel sure, the physical order too is really keeping time—they taste a larger life; more universal, more divine. As Plotinus said, they are looking at the Conductor in the midst; and, keeping time with Him, find the fulfilment both of their striving and of their peace.

THE PRICE OF LOVE

Note that this spiritual life which we have here considered is not an aristocratic life. It is a life of which the fundamentals are given by the simplest kinds of traditional piety, and have been exhibited over and over again by the simplest souls. An unconditioned self-surrender to the Divine Will, under whatever symbols it may be thought of; for we know that the very crudest of symbols is often strong enough to make a bridge between the heart and the Eternal and so be a vehicle of the Spirit of Life. A little silence and leisure. A great deal of faithfulness, kindness and courage. All this is within the reach of any one who cares enough for it to pay the price.

MAN'S CHIEF END

The first question is not 'What is best for my soul?' nor is it even 'What is most useful to humanity?' But—transcending both these limited aims—what function must this life fulfil in the great and secret economy of God? How directly and fully that principle admits us into the glorious liberty of the children of God; where we move with such ease and suppleness, because the whole is greater than any of its parts and in that whole we have forgotten ourselves.

Indeed, if God is All and His Word to us is All, that must mean that He is the reality and controlling factor of every situation, religious or secular; and that it is only for His glory and creative purpose that it exists. Therefore our favourite distinction between the spiritual life and the practical life is false. We cannot divide them. One affects the other all the time: for we are creatures of sense and of spirit and must lead an amphibious life. Christ's whole

Ministry was an exhibition, first in one way and then in another, of this mysterious truth. It is through all the circumstances of existence, inward and outward, not only those which we like to label spiritual, that we are pressed to our right position and given our supernatural food. For a spiritual life is simply a life in which all we do comes from the centre where we are anchored in God: a life soaked through and through by a sense of His reality and claim, and self-given to the great movement of His will.

THE UNCOMMON COMMONPLACE

To the eye of faith the common life of humanity, not any abnormal or unusual experience, is the material of God's redeeming action. As ordinary food and water are the stuff of the Christian sacraments, so it is in the ordinary pain and joy, tension and self-oblivion, sin and heroism of normal experience that His moulding and transfiguring work is known. The Palestinian glow which irradiates the homely mysteries of the Gospel, and gives to them the quality of eternal life, lights up for Faith the slums and suburbs, the bustle, games and industries of the modern world. Then the joys, sorrows, choices, renunciations, the poor little efforts and tragedies . . . are seen to be shot through, dignified and transfigured by heavenly radiance, self-oblivious heroism. Nor can we exclude from a share in this transforming glory the mystery and pathos of the animal creation from which our natural lives emerge. Faith shows us each tiny creature ringed round by celestial light. A deep reverence for our common existence with its struggles and faultiness, yet its solemn implications, comes over us when we realize all this; gratitude for the ceaseless tensions and opportunities through which God comes to us and we can draw a little nearer to Him—a divine economy in which the simplest and weakest are given their part and lot in the holy redemptive sacrifice of humanity and incorporated in the Mystical Body which incarnates Eternal Life.

IN LOVE WE LIVE

Our Lord found great significance in the life of birds; in their freedom, their self-abandoned trust, their release from mere carefulness. He held them precious to God, and patterns for the faith and hope of man. I sometimes think the divine gift of Hope—that confident tendency of the soul, that trust in the invisible, and in a real goal, a Country, truly awaiting us—poured into man by God to give meaning and buoyancy to his life: all this was first, as it were, tried out on birds. Long ages before we appeared, the clouds of tiny migrants swept over the face of this planet. Incarnate scraps of hope, courage, determination, they were ready at a given moment to leave all and follow the inward voice; obeying the instinct that called them in the teeth of peril and difficulty, giving themselves trustfully to the supporting air.

Nor does this exhaust their likeness to the soul. If we ask why the bird is so utterly at home . . . science replies that it is itself partly a creature of air. Its very bones are so made that the air penetrates and informs them. It is lifted from within as well as supported from without; the invisible Kingdom to which it gives itself is inseparably a part of its own life. Even so are we both penetrated and supported by an ocean of Love and Life; an infinite yet indwelling Reality experienced though unseen: 'God in Himself as He is everywhere and at all times' as St. Thomas has it. 'And now, what is my hope? surely my hope is in

Thee'—as the bird in the air, so we in the Being of God. As the bird we are called to another country, a *Patria*. The courage which can face long effort, vast and lonely distances, apparent emptiness, may be the testing condition of our flight. Yet the loneliness and emptiness are only apparent: for in Him we live and move and have our being, even while to Him we tend. He inspires and supports the adventure of which He is the goal. For Hope is Love, tending to God at all costs; bearing all things, believing all things, because sure that He has made us for Himself and our hearts shall find rest in Him alone.

EDUCATION FOR LOVE

Our aim ought to be to teach and impress the reality of Spirit, its regnancy in human life, whilst the mind is alert and supple: and so to teach and impress it, that it is woven into the stuff of the mental and moral life and cannot seriously be injured by the hostile criticisms of the rationalist. Remember that the prime object of education is the moulding of the unconscious and instinctive nature, the home of habit. If we can give this the desired tendency and tone of feeling, we can trust the rational mind to find good reasons with which to reinforce its attitudes and preferences. . . .

Did we know our business we surely ought to be able to ensure in our young people a steady and harmonious spiritual growth. The 'conversion' or psychic convulsion which is sometimes regarded as an essential preliminary of any vivid awakening of the spiritual consciousness is really a tribute exacted by our wrong educational methods. It is a proof that we have allowed the plastic creature confided to us, to harden in the wrong shape. But if, side by side, and in simplest language, we teach the conceptions:

first, of God as the transcendent yet indwelling Spirit of love, of beauty, and of power; next, of man's constant dependence on Him and possible contact with His nature in that arduous and loving act of attention which is the essence of prayer; last, of unselfish work and fellowship as the necessary expressions of human ideals—then, I think, we may hope to lay the foundations of a balanced and a wholesome life, in which man's various faculties work together for good, and his vigorous instinctive life is directed to the highest ends.

LIFE AND LOVE

(a) *What is Life?*

If we would read the secret of reality, we must read it as we run. Moreover, on this, our unarrested flight, we are always changing; and with that incessant change, constructing new images from the inflowing messages, sliding from old words to new, from old to new readings of reality. This process is beyond our control: we cannot slacken or accelerate our pace, stand and survey the landscape through which we are passing; we cannot look Eternity in the face. . . . This is the condition of that which Mr. Wells has called our 'reluctant and fugitive humanity'; and the problem of life, for those who are aware of it, becomes the problem of how best to use the measure of freedom which our condition involves. The mounting flood of life, the ceaseless stream of becoming, presses on and up, and we with it. How shall we go? 'Reluctant and fugitive' or gladly and with pride? Shall our divine faculty of conscious attention be given to the great purposes of the journey or to the little distractive incidents of the way? Shall we drift or march; be conscripts or volunteers? It is a forced option, and a vital one. The whole meaning of life depends for us on the choice that we make between the status of slave and son.

Life, the Spirit of Life, invites our love—a love industrious and courageous—and it is in generous and disinterested response to this invitation that man's happiness consists.

'The joy of the true lover is to serve him that he loveth.' To love life in this sense, with a love which gives but does not grasp, which co-operates eagerly and passionately in the hard and painful work that life must do, is the exact antithesis of loving 'the world.' It makes the man who has it, whether he dig the earth or search the stars, a partner in the business of the Universe: a voluntary instrument for the self-expression of the strong Spirit which is behind the appearance of things.

(b) The Divine Spirit of Life

St. Paul, that great gazer on reality, who has too long remained the exclusive property of the theologians, said of the society which he founded that it was a 'mystical body' of many members, which one living Spirit inhabited and transfused. So too, the whole of humanity is the mystical body of a Spirit—the stirring, unresting divine Spirit of Life. The individual man represents one more opportunity for this Spirit to break out in a fresh place, to new spontaneous manifestations of energy, beauty, endurance or love. He has a vocation as part of the veritable *Corpus Domini*. Those who accept this vocation laid on them, and rejoice in it, never shirking, turning on their tracks, or thwarting the movements of that deep interior tide, these are the truly successful and the truly glad. 'How hard it is for thee to kick against the pricks,' said the Voice on the way to Damascus: and stated in these words the law which governs all unhappiness.

The men who thus acquiesce in Life and offer her their love and service, find their advances met half-way. All things become friendly to them because they have been adopted into the mighty family of the Sons of God. In every living thing they discern the movement and self-expression of that Spirit which they serve. New kingdoms of life are disclosed to them: the Uncreated Light illuminates for them the most painfully artistic villas and the meanest streets. They feel, with that poignant emotion for which man has yet to find a name, the passionate vitality which burns in every blade of grass and budding spray. They perceive and worship, though they may not understand, the steady rhythm of growth by which they are surrounded, the perpetual unfolding of new beauty and new power: within themselves they feel the pulse of that same urgent Spirit, and know themselves to be concerned in the stupendous adventure of the Universe.

(c) *The Fullness of Life*

This life in intuitive sympathy with the Whole, or imaginative vision of the Real—oblique descriptions of one and the same state of consciousness—should surely lie across the 'practical' life of man, if that life is to have true significance, as the weft which gives pattern, colour and cohesion, lies across the warp which gives strength. By it the humble and meek are exalted, the proud put down; for it knits up each little life with the whole of life, makes each separate achievement—meaningless, perhaps sordid in itself—count in the infinitely romantic achievement of the All. By this way alone can we escape from that 'flame of separation' which the Sufis held to be the greatest of ills. This alone destroys the terrific loneliness of the self-conscious soul contemplating the Universe from within the prison of the flesh.

Greatest gain of all, this transfusing consciousness gives disinterestedness to man's life. In its light, the well-being of the whole is seen as the central fact for each separate existence: and thus it provides an antidote at once to the poison of success and to the bitterness of failure.

SAINTS AND MYSTICS, THE EXPONENTS OF LOVE

TRANSCENDENCE

Within thy sheltering darkness spin the spheres;
Within the shaded hollow of thy wings.
The life of things,
The changeless pivot of the passing years—
These in thy bosom lie.
Restless we seek thy being; to and fro
Upon our little twisting earth we go:
We cry, 'Lo, there!'
When some new avatar thy glory does declare,
When some new prophet of thy friendship sings,
And in his tracks we run
Like an enchanted child, that hastes to catch the sun.

And shall the soul thereby
Unto the All draw nigh?
Shall it avail to plumb the mystic deeps
Of flowery beauty, scale the icy steeps
Of perilous thought, the hidden Face to find,
Or tread the starry paths to the utmost verge of the sky?
Nay, groping dull and blind
Within the sheltering dimness of thy wings—
Shade that their splendour flings
Athwart Eternity—
We, out of age-long wandering, but come
Back to the Father's heart, where now we are at home.

THE SIGNIFICANCE OF A SAINT

WHAT is a Saint? A particular individual completely redeemed from self-occupation; who, because of this, is able to embody and radiate a measure of Eternal Life. His whole life, personal, social, intellectual, mystical, is lived in the supernatural regard. What is he for? To help, save, and enlighten by his loving actions and contemplations; to oppose in one way or another, by suffering, prayer and work upon heroic levels of love and self-oblation, the mysterious downward drag, within the world, which we call sin.

LOVE, THE SOUL OF SANCTITY

A saint is a human creature devoured and transformed by love: a love that has dissolved and burnt out those instinctive passions—acquisitive and combative, proud and greedy—which commonly rule the lives of men. Therefore we must always consider him in relation with the two supreme objects of his love; God and the World, or that special bit of the world on which he is destined to pour out his charity. The isolated facts about St. Francis . . . are all found when we examine them, to be simply different expressions . . . of that love which made of him, perhaps, the most unspoilt channel of the Divine generosity known to us since New Testament times. That outpouring Charity, that *Agape*, in which the manward life of God consists, transformed him by 'the kindling of his mind,' as he was told in the great experience on La Verna, so that his whole life . . . was swept up to become part of the Divine action, the self-expression of the Divine Love.

THE TOOL OF LOVE

Living with an intensity which entails for him the extremes of suffering and joy, the saint is always, at his full development, both active and contemplative—as indeed every living member of the Mystical Body is bound in some manner to be—giving in devoted service that which he receives in child-like prayer. This must be so, since for the Christian saint, union with God means union with One who is both here and there, both humble and Almighty, self-given and transcendent. Therefore it cannot mean mere flight from this world and its needs, or any other private satisfaction, however spiritual and exalted. The very genius of Christianity is generosity, *Agape*; and the saint stands out as the self-emptied channel of that supernatural Love. The rich, active life-giving character of Christian holiness depends directly on the Christian doctrine of the Nature of God. By that constant re-immersion in the atmosphere of Eternity, which is the essence of prayer, the Christian saint becomes able in his turn to radiate Eternity; and the more profound his contemplation, the more he loves the world, and tries to serve it as the tool of the Divine creative love . . . For he has become—and this is perhaps the most satisfactory of all our imperfect definitions—a 'pure capacity for God.'

THE DIFFERENTIA OF THE SAINTS

The saintly and simple Curé d'Ars was once asked the secret of his abnormal success in converting souls. He replied that it was done by being very indulgent to others and very hard on himself; a recipe which retains all its virtue still. And this power of being outwardly genial and inwardly austere, which is the real Christian temper, depends entirely on the use we make of the time set apart for personal religion. It is always achieved if courageously and faithfully sought; and there are no heights of love and holiness to which it cannot lead, no limits to the powers which it can exercise over the souls of men.

We have the saints to show us that these things are actually possible: that one human soul can rescue and transfigure another and can endure for it redemptive hardship and pain. We may allow that the saints are specialists; but they are specialists in a career to which all Christians are called. They have achieved the classic status. They are the advanced guard of the army; but we after all are marching in the main ranks. The whole army is dedicated to the same supernatural cause and we ought to envisage it as a whole, and to remember that every one of us wears the same uniform as the saints, has access to the same privileges, is taught the same drill and fed with the same food. The difference between them and us is a difference in degree, not in kind. They possess and we most conspicuously lack, a certain maturity and depth of soul; caused by the perfect flowering in them of self-oblivious love, joy and peace. We recognize in them a finished product, a genuine work of God. But this power and beauty of the saints is on the human side simply the result of their faithful life of prayer; and is something to which every Christian worker can attain. Therefore we ought all to be a little bit like them; to have a sort of family likeness to share the family point of view.

THE SOULS OF THE SAINTS

Nothing in all nature is so lovely and so vigorous, so perfectly at home in its environment, as a fish in the sea. Its surroundings give to it a beauty, quality, and power which is not its own. We take it out, and at once a poor, limp dull thing, fit for nothing, is gasping away its life. So the soul sunk in God, living the life of prayer, is supported, filled, transformed in beauty, by a vitality and a power which are not its own. The souls of the saints are so powerful because they are thus utterly immersed in the Spirit: their whole life is a prayer. The Life in which they live and move and have their being gives them something of its own quality. So long as they maintain themselves within it, they are adequate to its demands, because fed by its gifts. This re-entrance into our Origin and acceptance of our true inheritance is the supernatural life of prayer, as it may be experienced by the human soul. Far better to be a shrimp within that ocean, than a full-sized theological whale cast upon the shore.

ARTISTS OF ETERNAL LIFE

The saints and men and women of prayer to whom we owe our deepest revelations of the Supernatural—those who give us real news about God—are never untrained amateurs or prodigies. Such men and women as Paul, Augustine, Catherine, Julian, Ruysbroeck, are genuine artists of eternal life. They have accepted and not scorned the teachings of tradition: and humbly trained and disciplined their God-given genius for ultimates.

THE KNOWLEDGE OF THE MYSTICS

The mystics—to give them their short, familiar name— are men and women who insist that they know for certain the presence and activity of that which they call the Love of God. They are conscious of that Fact which is there for all, and which is the true subject-matter of religion;

but of which the average man remains either unconscious or faintly and occasionally aware. They know a spiritual order, penetrating, and everywhere conditioning though transcending the world of sense. They declare to us a Reality most rich and living, which is not a reality of time and space; which is something other than everything we mean by 'nature,' and for which no merely pantheistic explanation will suffice.

THE ACHIEVEMENT OF THE MYSTIC

As the ordinary man is the meeting-place between two stages of reality—the sense-world and the world of the spiritual life—so the mystic, standing head and shoulders above ordinary men, is again the meeting-place between two orders. Or, if you like it better, he is able to perceive and react to reality under two modes. On the one hand he knews and rests in the eternal world of Pure Being, the 'Sea Pacific' of the Godhead, indubitably present to him in his ecstasies, attained by him in the union of love. On the other, he knows—and works in—that 'stormy sea,' the vital World of Becoming which is the expression of Its will. 'Illuminated men,' says Ruysbroeck, 'are caught up above reason, into naked vision. There the Divine Unity dwells and calls them. Hence their bare vision, cleansed and free, penetrates the activity of all created things and pursues it to search it out even to its height.'

THE MYSTIC WAY

The mystic knows his task to be the attainment of Being, union with the One, the 'return to the Father's heart'; for the parable of the Prodigal Son is to him the history of the universe. This union is to be attained, first by co-operation in that Life which bears him up, in which he is immersed. He must become conscious of this 'great life of the All,' merge himself in it, if he would find his way back whence he came. *Vae soli.* Hence there are really two separate acts of 'divine union,' two separate kinds of illumination involved in the Mystic Way: the dual character of the spiritual consciousness brings a dual responsibility in its train. First, there is the union with Life, with the World of Becoming: and parallel with it the illumination by which the mystic 'gazes upon a more veritable world.' Secondly, there is the union with Being, with the One: and that final, ineffable illumination of pure love which is called 'the knowledge of God.' It is through the development of the third factor, the free, creative 'Spirit,' the scrap of Absolute Life, which is the ground of his soul, that the mystic can (*a*) conceive, and (*b*) accomplish these transcendent acts. Only Being can know Being: we 'behold that which we are and are that which we behold.' But there is a spark in man's soul, say the mystics, which is real—which in fact *is*—and by its cultivation, we may know reality.

MYSTICISM

Mysticism then is not an opinion; it is not a philosophy. It has nothing in common with the pursuit of occult knowledge. It is not merely the power of contemplating Eternity . . . It is the name of that organic process which involves the perfect consummation of the Love of God: the achievement here and now of the immortal heritage of man. Or, if you like it better—for this means exactly the same thing—it is the art of establishing his conscious relation with the Absolute.

THE ESSENTIAL LINK

True mystical achievement is the most complete and most difficult expression of life which is as yet possible to man. It is at once an act of love, an act of surrender, and an act of supreme perception; a trinity of experiences which meets and satisfies the three activities of the self. Religion might give us the first and metaphysics the third of these processes. Only Mysticism can offer the middle term of the series, the essential link which binds the three in one. 'Secrets,' says St. Catherine of Siena, 'are revealed to a friend who has become *one thing* with his friend, and not to a servant.'

THE MYSTIC'S WITNESS

The note is never, '*I* have seen,' but always '*We* shall or may see.' Such an objective mystic as this, who is not content with retailing his private experiences and ecstasies, but accepts the great vocation of revealer of Reality, is called upon to do certain things. He must give us, not merely a static picture of Eternity, but also a dynamic 'reading of life'; and of a life more extended than that which the moralist, or even the philosopher, offers to interpret. He must not only tell us what he thinks about the universe, and in particular that ultimate Spiritual Reality which all mysticism discerns within or beyond the flux. He must also tell us what he thinks of man, that living, moving, fluid spirit-thing: his reactions to this universe and this Reality, the satisfaction which it offers to his thought, will and love, the obligations laid upon him in respect of it. We, on our part, must try to understand what he tells us of these things; for he is, as it were, an organ developed by the race for this purpose—a tentacle pushed out towards the infinite, to make in our name and in our interest, fresh contacts with Reality. He performs for us some of the functions of the artist extending our universe, the pioneer cutting our path, the hunter winning food for our souls.

The clue to the universe of such a mystic will always be the vision or idea which he has of the Nature of God; and there we must begin if we would find our way through the tangle of his thought. From this Centre all else branches out, and to this all else must conform, if it is to have for him realness and life, for truth, as Aquinas teaches, is simply the reality of things as they are in God.

THE MYSTIC'S UNIVERSE

Mystics, philosophers and artists

As only the wide-open aesthetic faculty of the great artist seems able to perceive and exhibit to us a sense-world which is truly adequate to our cravings; and only the profound intellect of the great philosopher can satisfy the insistent demands of reason for a rational universe, so only the intuition of the great mystics seems able to know and give to others in some measure, a spiritual universe and reality which is convincing, all-demanding, utterly satisfying in its dimly felt and solemn spacelessness, its thrilling attraction and aliveness. . . .

Thus, as from the great poet we learn the full possibilities and the transcendency of Poetry, it is from the saint that we learn the full possibilities and transcendency of Religion.

PRAYER, THE COMMERCE OF LOVE

PRAYER

In the triumph of prayer
Twofold is the spell.
With the folding of hands
There's a spreading of wings
And the soul's lifted up to invisible lands
And ineffable peace. Yet it knows, being there
That it's close to the heart of all pitiful things;
And it loses and finds, and it gives and demands;
For its life is divine, it must love, it must share
In the triumph of prayer.

In the anguish of prayer
It is well! It is well!
Then only the victory of love is complete,
When the soul on the cross
Dies to all save its loss.
When in utmost defeat
The light that was fair
And the friend who was sweet
Flee away, then the truth of its love is laid bare
In the anguish of prayer.

HIGH TIDE

Flood thou my soul with thy great quietness,
O let thy wave
Of silence from the deep
Roll in on me, the shores of sense to lave:

So doth thy living water softly creep
Into each cave
And rocky pool, where ocean creatures hide
Far from their home, yet nourished by thy tide.
Deep sunk they wait
The coming of thy great
Inpouring stream that shall new life communicate;
Then, starting from beneath some shadowy ledge
Of the heart's edge,
Flash sudden coloured memories of the sea
Whence they were born of thee
Across the mirrored surface of the mind.
Swift rays of wondrousness
They seem;
And rippling thoughts arise
Fan-wise
From the quick-darting passage of the dream,
To spread and find
Each creviced narrowness
Where the dark waters dwell,
Mortally still
Until
The Moon of prayer,
That by the invincible sorcery of love
God's very self can move,
Draws thy life-giving flood
E'en there.
Then the great swell
And urge of grace
Refresh the weary mood;
Cleansing anew each sad and stagnant place
That seems shut off from thee,
And hardly hears the murmur of the sea.

ENRICHMENT of the sense of God is surely the crying need of our current Christianity. A shallow religiousness, the tendency to be content with a bright ethical piety wrongly called practical Christianity . . . seems to me one of the defects of institutional religion at the present time. We are drifting towards a religion which consciously or unconsciously keeps its eye on humanity rather than on Deity—which lays all the stress on service and hardly any of the stress on awe: and that is a type of religion which in practice does not wear well. It does little for the soul in those awful moments when the pain and mystery of life are most deeply felt. It does not provide a place for that profound experience which Tauler calls 'suffering in God.' It does not lead to sanctity: and sanctity after all is the religious goal. It does not fit those who accept it as adequate for the solemn privilege of guiding souls to God . . . In fact it turns its back on the most profound gifts made by Christianity to the human race. I do not think we can deny that there is . . . a definite trend in the direction of religion of this shallow social type . . . It will only be checked in so far as the clergy are themselves real men of prayer. Therefore to become and continue a real man of prayer, seems to me the first duty of a parish priest.

What is a real man of prayer? He is one who deliberately wills and steadily desires that his intercourse with God and other souls shall be controlled and actuated at every point by God Himself; one who has so far developed and educated his spiritual sense that his supernatural environment is more real and solid than his natural environment. A man of prayer is not necessarily a person who says a

number of offices or abounds in detailed intercessions;
but he is a child of God who is and knows himself to be
in the deeps of his soul attached to God and is wholly and
entirely guided by the Creative Spirit in his prayer and his
work. This is not merely a bit of pious language. It is a
description . . . of the only real apostolic life. Every
Christian starts with a chance of it; but only a few develop
it. The laity distinguish in a moment the clergy who have it
from the clergy who have it not: there is nothing you can
do for God or for the souls of men which exceeds in importance the achievement of that spiritual temper and attitude.

SPIRITUAL SYMPHONY

Since the vocation of each soul within that great
symphony differs, and all are needed for the complete
expression of the thought of God, we need not be surprised
by the wide diversities, or even the apparent contradictions
in *attrait* and in practice, which are found in the world of
prayer. We are not to criticize our neighbour's mono-
tonous performance on the triangle, censure the first
violin's deliberate silence, or look dubiously at the little
bit of score we have received. All contribute to one only
music; and this alone gives meaning to their prayer. 'This
it is that I ask and desire,' says Thomas à Kempis, 'that I
may always laud and praise Thee.' Some will do this above
all in the upward glance of an adoring worship, some by a
more intimate love, some by the small offerings of a
devoted industry.

THE SPIRIT OF PRAYER

The maintaining of the spirit of prayer and waiting on
God is one of the greatest things Christians can do to help

the world. We must each take our part in it and learn to do it as well as we can. Even in war and dispeace we can keep the Peace of God in our hearts and share it with others, but only if we keep in constant and loving remembrance of Him, dwell on the unchanging Peace, Holiness and Beauty of God and lift up our hearts and minds to Him in a short prayer, such as:

> *Praise the Lord, O my soul!*
> *Give us, O Lord, the spirit of Faith, Hope and Charity!*
> *Thy service is perfect freedom!*
> *Give me Thy Spirit of Patience and Love!*
> *Into Thy hands, O Lord, I commend my spirit.*

THE HEART OF PRAYER

In all its degrees, from the most naïve to the most transcendental, and in all its expressions—from the most simple and homely devotional acts, to that passive waiting on the Spirit, 'idle in appearance, and yet so active,' which is called by Grou 'the adoration most worthy of God'— the very heart of prayer is this opening up of human personality to the all-penetrating and all-purifying Divine activity. On one hand, we acknowledge our need and our dependence; on the other the certain presence of the supernatural world, the *Patria* ever in intimate contact with us, and our own possession of a seed, a supernatural spark, which knows that world and corresponds with it. Thus all progress in prayer, whatever its apparent form or achievements, consists in the development of this, its essential character. It must nourish and deepen our humility, confidence and love; and thus set up and maintain an ever more perfect commerce between the soul's true being and that Being in Whom it lives and moves. This is why, in the concrete reality of the interior life, prayer and purification must always go hand in hand.

TRANSCENDENT AND IMMANENT

It is the special function of prayer to turn the self away from the time-series and towards the eternal order; away from the apparent and towards the significant; away from succession and towards adoration and adherence. Prayer opens the door of the psyche to the invasion of another order, which shall at its full term transform the very quality of our existence. And Spirit, in its most general sense, is our name for that world, life, Being, which is then apprehended by us; and for that quality in ourselves which is capable of such apprehension and response. Moreover, this sacred category, lying behind the native land of the intelligence, is not to be thought of lightly, vaguely or coldly as mere material for academic speculation. We do not mean by it some tenuous region or plane to which physical considerations cannot apply. The whole witness of religion suggests that it is alive with an awful splendour, a range of personal action, which extends from the most tender and intimate workings on the individual soul, to the inconceivable energies and secret movements which can sometimes be detected behind the pageant of the visible world.

FLOWER AND SEED

In studying prayer, it is surely, above all, important to look at the flower and not at the seed. A very rough little seed, buried deep in the primitive stuff of human nature, and finding its first nourishment in our primitive terrors and needs; a flower, of which we cannot yet analyse the mysterious fragrance or estimate the healing power. Even though its first beginnings and first enticements are naïve and humble—wholly utilitarian in their objectives, and largely dictated by the ignoble passions of fear and desire—this embryonic movement towards communion with the invisible Other must surely be judged, as we judge the beginnings of architecture, painting and music, in relation with its triumphant developments. The mud hut does not discredit the cathedral; nor does the devotee of Durga discredit the adoring prayer of the saints.

In Him life lay, and this life was the Light for men! Amid the darkness the Light shone, but the darkness did not master it.[1]

CREATIVE PROCESS

Prayer is the substance of eternal life. It gives back to man, in so far as he is willing to live to capacity—that is to say, to give love and suffer pain—the beatitude without which he is incomplete; for it sets going, deepens and at last perfects that mutual indwelling of two orders which redeems us from unreality, and in which the creative process reaches its goal.

PROGRESS IN PRAYER

Do not entertain the notion that you ought to *advance* in your prayer. If you do, you will only find you have put on the brake instead of the accelerator. All real progress in spiritual things comes gently, imperceptibly, and is the work of God. Our crude efforts spoil it. Know yourself for the childish, limited and dependent soul you are. Remember that the only growth which matters happens

[1] St. John i. 4, 5. Moffatt's translation.

without our knowledge and that trying to stretch ourselves
is both dangerous and silly. Think of the Infinite Goodness,
never of your own state. Realize that the very capacity
to pray at all is the free gift of the Divine Love and be
content with St. Francis de Sales' favourite prayer in which
all personal religion is summed up. 'Yes, Father! Yes and
always Yes!' . . .

Let us rejoice in the great adoring acts and splendid
heroisms of God's great lovers and humbly do the little
bit we can. We too have our place.

ARDOUR AND BEAUTY

Love should give two things to prayer; ardour and beauty.
In his prayer, as it were, man swings a censer before the
altar of the universe. He may put into the thurible all his
thoughts and dreams, all his will and energy. But unless the
fire of love is communicated to that incense, nothing will
happen; there will be no fragrance and no ascending smoke.
These qualities—ardour and beauty—represent two distinct
types of feeling, which ought both to find a place in the
complete spiritual life, balancing and completing one
another. The first is in the highest degree intimate and
personal; the second is disinterested and aesthetic.

(a) ADORATION

NEBULA AND NEST

I

I have fled far!
I have not stayed my quest for any star
That in my pathway stood
And sang in the soul's ear
'Behold the Good!'
But I have sought the sphere
Wherein his thought immense—
His love, his dream,
His ardent seeking sense
Of uttermost exactitudes that seem
All novelty and flow and wilful change
Crest upward first toward creative joy:
And from the dreadful range
Of absolute and unconditioned Mind
Door of deliverance find
In sweet employ.

I stretched upon his storm my fragile wings,
And went with the great wind
That poured its music through the frame of things.
Dreadful was the embrace
To which we rushed beyond the edge of space:
For he that is all-loving would immerse
His fulhead in the Nought
His immemorial thought
Utter through strife.
Yea! as melodic fire
That sought the consummation of desire

All down the exultant trumpet of the skies
Athwart the spreaded strings
Of vibrant light
There was our flight,
And as a speedful song was our emprize.

So have I seen the sacred stream of life
In one swift act sublime
Enter our universe;
The bridal of eternity and time.
Then in the womb of darkness there began
Soft movements of maternal energy,
And golden filaments of life that ran
Athwart the dim.
Then first was laid the plan
That builded upward to the soul of man
And bore to him
Far in the wild
A veritable child.

II

Yea, I have travelled far,
I have not stayed my quest for any star
Nor found in any sun the light I need:
Authentic converse with the unconfined
This might alone suffice mine avid mind,
This might alone my hungry spirit feed.
Now in and in I come,
Out of the mists of distant nebulæ
Swing again home:
Entering at last,
The edgeless solitudes of God o'erpassed,

That one warm narrow place
Where mind is free
From the terrific liberties of space
And the heart best
Can make for him a nest.
And as the palmer, coming home again
From the sweet Sepulchre,
Finds Christ afield amongst his fellow men
And summed in her
Who waits him, all his portion of that grace
Which shone from Mary's face:
So the pale skies
All lucent with God's love
And the swift cloudy spirits that arise
Wistful of some unthought divine surprise
Full friendly prove
To this my quest, and heal my hungry pain.
Yet softly say, 'In vain
Thy pilgrim's scrip and all thy traveller's state.
As we around the earth in pageant go
Yet to no goal attain,
Thou dost but tread the orbit of thy brain
In thine ecstatic flight
That would achieve his dread excess of bright.
Not so
The limited, the Limitless may know.
Wait, pilgrim, wait!
Cleanse thou thy sight,
Prepare thine ear,
To see him in his light,
The flowering of his melody to hear
His feet are on the road: stay thou at home.
He shall appoint a meeting when he come.'

III

How still it is!
And yet there's music here,
Music alone goes with me all the way
Divinely clear.
Thou dost beat out at me
From the leaves of the chestnut tree,
Here at my window peeping as I pray,
The very Self-hood's bliss
In life's rich fugue confessed;
Thy heart's dear melody
By crescent form expressed.
And I, that all the fervours of the abyss
Might not delay,
Am caught in thy bird's nest—
Meet shelter of the smallest soul that sings—
Find, nestling warm against a feathery breast,
My long-sought rest,
And fold my weary wings.

THE PRIMACY OF ADORATION

ADORATION is the first and greatest of life's responses to its spiritual environment; the first and most fundamental of spirit's movements towards Spirit, the seed from which all other prayer must spring. It is among the most powerful of the educative forces which purify the understanding, form and develop the spiritual life. As we can never know the secret of great art or music until we have learned to look and listen with a self-oblivious reverence, acknowledging a beauty that is beyond our grasp—so the claim and loveliness remain unrealized till we have learned to look, to listen, to adore. Then only do we go beyond ourselves and our small vision, pour ourselves out to that which we know not, and so escape from our own pettiness and limitations into the universal life.

THE INCLUSIVENESS OF ADORATION

What really seems to matter most? The perfection of His mighty Symphony, or your own remarkably clever performance of that difficult passage for the tenth violin? And again, if the music unexpectedly requires your entire silence, which takes priority in your feelings? The mystery and beauty of God's orchestration? Or the snub administered to you? Adoration, widening our horizons, drowning our limited interests in the total interests of Reality, redeems the spiritual life from all religious pettiness and gives it a wonderful richness, meaning and span. And more: every aspect, even the most homely, of our practical life can become part of this adoring response, this total life; and always has done in those who have achieved full spiritual

133

personality. *All the earth doth worship Thee*, means what it says. The life, beauty and meaning of the whole created order, from the tomtit to the Milky Way, refers back to the Absolute Life and Beauty of its Creator; and so perceived, so lived, every bit has spiritual significance. Thus the old woman of the legend could boil her potatoes to the greater glory of God; and St. Teresa, taking her turn in the kitchen, found Him very easily among the pots and pans.

THE FIRST MOOD OF PRAYER

If the first term of the spiritual life is recognition in some way or other of the splendour and reality of God, the first mood of prayer—the ground from which all the rest must grow—is certainly worship, awe, adoration; delight in that holy reality for its own sake. This truth has lately returned to the foreground of religious thought; and there is little need to insist on it afresh. Religion, as von Hügel loved to say, *is* adoration; man's humble acknowledgement of the Transcendent, the Fact of God—the awestruck realism of the seraphs in Isaiah's vision—the meek and loving sense of mystery which enlarges the soul's horizon and puts us in our own place. Prayer, which is so much more a state and condition of soul than a distinct act, begins there; in the lifting of the eyes of the little creature to the Living God, or perhaps to the symbol through which the Living God reveals Himself to the soul.

THE HEART OF PRAYER

Adoration ... must be the very heart of the life of prayer. For prayer is a supernatural activity or nothing at all; and it must primarily be directed to supernatural ends. It, too, acknowledges the soul's basic law: it comes from God, belongs to God, is destined for God. It must begin, end, and be enclosed in the atmosphere of adoration; aiming at God for and in Himself. Our ultimate effect as transmitters of the supernal light and love directly depends on this adoring attentiveness. In such a prayer . . . we open our doors wide to receive His ever-present Spirit; abasing ourselves and acknowledging our own nothingness. Only the soul that has thus given itself to God becomes part of the mystical body through which He acts on life. Its destiny is to be the receiver and transmitter of grace. . . . Only when our souls are filled to the brim can we presume to offer spiritual gifts to other men. The remedy for that sense of impotence, that desperate spiritual exhaustion which religious workers too often know, is . . . an inner life governed not by petition but by adoring prayer. When we find that the demands made upon us are seriously threatening our inward poise, when we feel symptoms of starvation and stress, we can be quite sure that it is time to call a halt; to re-establish the fundamental relation of our souls with Eternal Reality, the Home and Father of our spirits. 'Our hearts shall have *no* rest save in Thee.' It is only when our hearts are thus actually at rest in God, in peaceful and self-oblivious adoration, that we can hope to show His attractiveness to other men.

THE ATTITUDE OF SOUL

Consider for a moment what the word Adoration implies. The upward and outward look of humble and joyful admiration. Awestruck delight in the splendour and beauty of God, the action of God and Being of God in and for Himself alone, as the very colour of life: giving its quality of unearthly beauty to the harshest, most disconcerting forms and the dreariest stretches of experience. This is adoration: not a difficult religious exercise, but an attitude of the soul. 'To Thee I lift up mine eyes, O Thou that dwellest in the heavens!': I don't turn round and look at myself. Adoration begins to purify us from egotism straight away. It may not always be easy—in fact for many people it is not at all easy—but it is realism; the atmosphere within which alone the spiritual life can be lived. *Our Father which art in Heaven, hallowed be Thy Name!*—That tremendous declaration, with its unlimited confidence and unlimited awe, governs everything else.

THE PRIORITY OF GOD

From first to last self-regarding elements are mixed with human worship; but these are no real part of it . . . 'Wherein does your prayer consist?' said St. John of the Cross to one of his penitents. She replied: 'In considering the Beauty of God and in rejoicing that He has such beauty' . . . Such disinterested delight is the perfection of worship . . . 'God,' says St. John of the Cross again, 'passes through the thicket of the world and wherever His glance falls, He turns all things to beauty.' . . .

Worship, then, at every level, always means God and the priority of God, however thick the veils through which He is apprehended, and however grotesque the disguise He may seem to wear. Through and in a multitude of strange divinities and along lowly channels suited to the lowliness of man, the 'outpouring of the Incomprehensible Grandeur,' as Dionysius the Areopagite says, goes on. We in our worshipping action are compelled to move within the devotional sphere, with all its symbolic furniture, its archaic survival, its pitfalls, its risks of sentimentalism,

herd-suggestion and disguised self-regard. But the mighty
Object of our worship stands beyond and over against all
this in His utter freedom and distinctness. 'Can' and
'cannot,' 'is' and 'is not' must not be predicated of Him,
without a virtual remembrance that these words merely
refer to our limited experience and not to God as He is
in Himself. If this contrast is forgotten, we shall never
understand the religious scene and the strange objects with
which it is bestrewn. There is no department of life which
asks from those who study it so much humble sympathy,
such a wide, genial, unfastidious spirit, or so constant a
remembrance of our own limitations as this; nor one in
which it is more necessary to remember the wholesome
reminder of the psychologists, that we ourselves, however
apparently civilized, are still possessed of a primitive sub-
consciousness which is nowhere more active than in the
practice of our religion.

THE SEED OF SUPERNATURAL LIFE

Worship purifies, enlightens, and at last transforms, every
life submitted to its influence: and this not merely in the
ethical or devotional sense. It does all this, because it
wakes up and liberates that 'seed' of supernatural life, in
virtue of which we are spiritual beings capable of responding to that God Who is Spirit; and which indeed gives to
humanity a certain mysterious kinship with Him. Worship
is therefore in the deepest sense creative and redemptive.
Keeping us in constant remembrance of the Unchanging
and the Holy, it cleanses us of subjectivism, releases us
from 'use and wont' and makes us realists. God's invitation
to it and man's response, however limited, crude or mistaken
this response may be, are the appointed means whereby we
move towards our true destiny.

ADORATION, THE SOURCE OF SANCTITY

Being, after all, at best half animal creatures, with a psychic machinery mainly adapted to maintaining our physical status, we cannot conceive a supernatural status and activity—much less achieve it—by ourselves. Until that secret holy energy we call 'grace' has touched and stirred us, we do not know what 'grace' is: it is a pious word, not the name of an actual power, a free gift from the sources of Eternal Life. And unless grace continues to play upon and support us, we cannot go on knowing what it is. Therefore attention to God, adoration of God, spreading gradually from its focus in deliberate devotional acts till it colours all the activities of existence, and from His discovery and worship under particular attributes to a certain tasting of Him as He is in Himself; this must be the first and governing term of the supernatural life, the unique source of all its possibilities. The reason the saints are so winning and persuasive, and so easily bring us into the presence of God, is that their lives are steeped in this loving and selfless adoration.

WORSHIP, THE CONDITION OF EFFECTIVENESS

Whole-hearted adoration is the only real preparation for right action: action which develops within the Divine atmosphere, and is in harmony with the eternal purposes of God. The Bible is full of illustrations of this truth, from the call of Isaiah to the Annunciation. First the awestruck recognition of God: and then, the doing of His Will. We cannot discern His Eternal Purpose, even as it affects our tiny lives, opportunities and choices, except with the eyes of disinterested and worshipping love. The hallowing of the Name is therefore the essential condition without which it is not possible to work for the Kingdom or recognize the pressure of the Will. So the first imperative of the life of prayer is that which the humanist finds so hard to understand. We are to turn our backs upon earth, and learn how to deal with its sins and its needs by looking steadfastly up to heaven.

ADORATION AND SELF-OFFERING

The prayer of adoration must end on the cry of St. Augustine: 'Lord, I seek not to penetrate Thy lofty nature, for in no way do I compare my understanding with it.' For the more deeply we enter the worshipping life, the more profoundly we experience the transcendence and the otherness of That which we adore; and the more deeply purifying is the failure of our understanding before the reality of God. And were this meek, objective worship the beginning and end of our relation with Reality, the note of ceaseless joy on which the Golden Sequence closes could never be heard in human prayer. But all is not over, because the Radiance that attracts also daunts us, and one side of our response to Spirit must always be a humble acknowledgement of our ignorance and nothingness before the rich simplicity of God. For that rich simplicity has a certain kinship with the creature, which It is ever moulding and creating both from without and within. Spirit indwells and penetrates the soul's very fabric as a quiet Love: and it is here, in our ground, that we are to experience the most intimate and transforming realities of Prayer. Here we may come to know by the penetration of the heart, that which we can never understand by the exercise of the mind.

For the life of prayer, in its full and balanced development, unites a width and depth of vision with a great interior dependence and intimacy. The vision of God and the love of God complete each other; one expands and enlightens, the other humbles, deepens and enslaves the soul. So long as we are human, both thought and feeling must enter into our response to surrounding realities; and in the life of prayer this thought and feeling touched by the Supernatural, become transformed into a great awe and a great love. Thus the prayer of adoration passes almost insensibly into the prayer of communion and self-offering, as worship becomes more realistic, more deeply coloured by love. Indeed it has sometimes been said that adoration and self-giving cover the whole ground of human prayer.

(b) COMMUNION

INVITATORY

Come! break thy fast,
Dear Heart, poor wearied one!
Long is the desert way thou hast to tread
Ere all be done,
The House of the Beloved attained at last.
See, here is angel's bread,
An earnest of that grace
My Bride shall have when this lorn way is trod,
And she beholds my face,
Her Lover and her God.

'Ashes thou art, to ashes shalt return,'
I said in anger. Thou didst answer, 'Yea!
Yet in these ashes still a fire doth burn
That shall outlive the clay
And drives me hence,
Purged by the ritual of penitence,
To wander lonely.' 'Nay,'
I said, 'Not all the way
In solitude, for I will surely come—
I, with my wounded feet,—
Far into this world's wilderness to meet
My Sister and my Bride;
That we may go together, side by side,
To the desired threshold of our home.
There, even upon the brink
Of our transcendent nuptials, thou shalt drink
Deep from the honied chalice of my pain.
Then shall I cry, 'Come! Bride and Pilgrim, rest,

Thy head upon Love's breast,
Where long thy griefs have lain,
—Dear child, poor wearied one!—
For Earth's long Lent is done;
The Easter of thy soul hath dawned at last.
Come! at Love's mystic table break thy fast.'

INTROVERSION

What do you seek within, O Soul, my Brother?
   What do you seek within?
I seek a life that shall never die,
   Some haven to win
   From mortality.

What do you find within, O Soul, my Brother?
   What do you find within?
I find great quiet where no noises come.
   Without, the world's din:
   Silence in my home.

Whom do you find within, O Soul, my Brother?
   Whom do you find within?
I find a friend that in secret came:
   His scarred hands within
   He shields a faint flame.

What would you do within, O Soul, my Brother?
   What would you do within?
Bar door and window that none may see:
   That alone we may be
   (Alone face to face,
   In that flame-lit place!)
   When first we begin
To speak one with another.

BECAUSE prayer is indeed a supernatural act, a movement of spirit towards Spirit, it is an act in which the natural creature can never begin or complete in his own power. Though it seems to him to be by his own free choice and movement that he lifts up his soul towards God, it is in truth this all-penetrating God, Who by His secret humble pressure stirs man to make this first movement of will and love. The apparent spontaneity, the exercise of our limited freedom—genuinely ours, and most necessary to the soul's health—are yet entirely dependent on this prevenient and overruling Presence, acting with power and gentleness in the soul's ground. Progress in prayer is perhaps most safely measured by our increasing recognition of this action, the extent in which Spirit 'prays in us' and we co-operate with it: till, in the apparently passive and yet most powerful prayer of the great contemplative, the consciousness of our own busy activity is entirely lost in the movement of the Divine will, and the soul is well content to 'let another act in her.'

RESPONSE OF THE SELF

This response . . . seems to the soul the response of a person to a Person. We find in it a touching utilization of all the simplest aspects of man's emotional life. Here the childlike come to their own and achieve a closeness of communion with Reality unreached by the loftiest thought. The little creature is met on its own level; the spirit that was first filled with awestruck worship is sought and won on its own ground. A strange and penetrating intercourse is established. Maintained by periods of concentrated and loving attention in which the self 'meditates,' 'contemplates,' or 'waits upon God' according to the measure of its powers, this gradually spreads to permeate the deeds of active life: bringing all external action into direct relationship with His Reality. Life is more and more felt in every detail to be overruled by the intimate and cherishing action of God; opening paths, suggesting sacrifices, bringing about those unforeseen events and relationships which condition the soul's advance.

RECEPTIVITY

The supreme act of communion, which bridges the gap between the finite and the infinite life, whilst it demands the co-operation of will and sense, is independent of thought and of feeling. At the apex of sacramental experience the soul is not dazzled by some overwhelming disclosure of Reality. She finds a gift of God proportionate to her situation, which asks of her nothing but a docile receptivity. He who clothes the lilies and feeds the birds will now, by the imperceptible action of His providence, ministered for the most part through earthly accidents, feed and keep her upon the levels of eternal life.

SURRENDER

Prayer is man's nearest approach to absolute action; it means the closest association of which any soul is at any time capable with the living and everywhere present God Who is the true initiator of all that we really do. Progress in it is really a progressive surrender of the conditioned creature to that unconditioned yet richly personal Reality, Who is the only source, teacher and object of prayer. Its whole wonder and mystery abide in this: that here our tiny souls are being invited and incited to communion with God, the Eternal Spirit of the Universe.

THE MUTUALITY OF PRAYER

Real prayer is a mutual act. It is that correspondence between our dependent spirits and His Absolute Spirit, worked partly by grace, but also partly by our wills which is our mysterious privilege as living children of the Spirit of all spirits, God. This deep communion, this 'prayer which is ceaseless,' continues without interruption in the ground of the loving soul.

FELLOWSHIP WITH GOD AND MAN

The prevenience of God is the dominant fact of all life; and therefore of the life of prayer. We, hard and loveless, already stand in heaven. We open the stiff doors of our hearts and direct our fluctuating wills to a completely present Love and Will, directing, moulding and creating us. One aspect of redemption and one meaning of the incarnate life of Christ is to show men how to love this Present God; Who comes to us in this thing and that thing, yet Who induces in us a thirst and a longing that cannot be satisfied by any other thing than Himself alone.

And, moreover, in these first words (our Father), the praying soul accepts once for all its true status as a member of the whole family of man. Our Father. It can never again enter into prayer as a ring-fenced individual, intent on a private relation with God; for this is a violation of the law of Charity. Its prayer must overflow the boundaries of self-hood to include the life, the needs of the race; accepting as a corollary of its filial relation with God, a brotherly relation with all other souls however diverse, and at every point replacing 'mine' with 'ours.' This widespreading love, this refusal of private advantage is the very condition of Christian prayer; for that prayer is an instrument of redemptive action, not merely of personal achievement.

PERSEVERING PRAYER

The life of communion which conversion sets going, the humble and arduous year by year acceptance and using of every experience in supernatural regard: this it is which gradually converts the penitent into the saint, as a real garden is made, not by sticking in plants, but by long and unremitting cultivation of the soil.

TRANSFORMING POWER

It is in the humble yet intimate, ardent yet little understood communion of the small human self with a present and infinite Companion . . . that the transforming power exercised by prayer on human personality is most clearly seen. Here some measure of the supernatural with its generous grace and beauty, its demand for self-donation, truly enters the life of every awakened soul. In all its degrees and kinds from the colloquy or free conversation 'as one friend with another' which results from meditation faithfully performed, through that gradual expansion and simplification of consciousness which leads to the silent yet deeply active absorption of the Prayer of Simplicity or of Quiet, this secret intercourse has marked educative and purifying effects.

(c) CONTEMPLATION

REGNUM CAELORUM VIM PATITUR

When our five-angled spears, that pierced the world
And drew its life-blood, faint before the wall
Which hems its secret splendour—when we fall,
Lance broken, banner furled,
Before that calm invincible defence
Whereon our folly hurled
The piteous armies of intelligence—
Then, oftentimes, we know
How conquering mercy to the battlefield
Comes through the darkness, freely to bestow
The prize for which we fought
Not knowing what we sought,
And salve the wounds of those who would not yield.

He loves the valiant foe; he comes not out to meet
The craven soul made captive of its fear:
Not these the victories that to him are sweet!
But the impetuous soldiery of truth,
And knighthood of the intellectual quest,
Who ask not for his ruth
Nor would desire his rest:
These are to him most dear,
And shall in their surrender yet prevail.
Yea! at the end of unrewarded days,
By swift and secret ways
As on a sudden moonbeam shining clear,
Soft through the night shall slide upon their gaze
The thrice-defended vision of the Grail:

And when his peace hath triumphed, these shall be
The flower of his celestial chivalry.

And did you think, he saith,
As to and fro he goes the trenches through,
My heart impregnable, that you must bring
The ballisters of faith
Their burning bolts to fling,
And all the cunning intricate device
Of human wit,
One little breach to make
That so you might attain to enter it?
Nay, on the other side
Love's undefended postern is set wide:
But thus it is I woo
My dearest sons, that an ignoble ease
Shall never please,
Nor any smooth and open way entice.
Armed would I have them come
Against the mighty bastions of their home;
Out of high failure win
Their way within,
And from my conquering hand their birthright take.

THE GATEWAY OF CONTEMPLATION

THE act of contemplation is for the mystic a psychic gateway; a method of going from one level of consciousness to another . . . That there is such a characteristic outlook is proved by the history of mysticism which demonstrates plainly enough that in some men another sort of consciousness, another 'sense' may be liberated beyond the normal powers . . . This 'sense' has attachments to emotion, to intellect and to will . . . Yet it differs from and transcends the emotional, intellectual and volitional life of ordinary men. It was recognized by Plato as that consciousness which could apprehend the real world of the Ideas. . . . It is called by Plotinus 'Another intellect, different from that which reasons . . .'. It is the sense which, in the words of the *Theologica Germanica* 'has the power of seeing into eternity,' the 'mysterious eye of the soul' by which St. Augustine saw 'the light that never changes.' In the words of St. Bernard it may be defined as 'the soul's unerring intuition, the unhesitating apprehension of truth'; which simple vision of truth, says St. Thomas Aquinas, 'ends in a movement of desire.'

It is infused with burning love, for it seems to its possessors to be primarily a movement of the heart: with intellectual subtlety, for its ardour is wholly spent upon the most sublime object of thought: with unflinching will, for its adventures are undertaken in the teeth of the natural doubts, prejudices, languors and self-indulgence of man . . . They are the only known methods by which we can come into concious possession of all our powers; and rising from the lower to the higher levels of consciousness, become aware of that larger life in which we are immersed, attain communion with the transcendent Personality in Whom that life is resumed.

Mary has chosen the better, not the idler part; for her gaze is directed towards those First Principles without which the activity of Martha would have no meaning at all. . . . It remains a paradox of the mystics that the passivity at which they appear to aim is really a state of the most intense activity: more, that where it is wholly absent no great creative action can take place. In it, the superficial self compels it to be still, in order that it may liberate another more deep-seated power which is, in the ecstasy of the contemplative genius, raised to the highest pitch of efficiency.

'This restful travail,' said Walter Hilton,[1] 'is full far from fleshly idleness and from blind security. It is full of ghostly work, but it is called rest, for grace looseth the heavy yoke of fleshly love from the soul and maketh it mighty and free through the gift of the holy ghostly love for to work gladly, softly, and delectably . . . Therefore is it called a holy idleness and a rest most busy; and so is it in *stillness* from the great crying and noise of fleshly desires.'

A MENTAL ATTITUDE

Contemplation . . . is a power which we may—and often must—apply to the perception, not only of Divine Reality, but of anything. It is a mental attitude under which all things give up to us the secret of their life. All artists are of necessity in some measure contemplative. In so far as they surrender themselves without selfish preoccupation, they see Creation from the point of view of God. 'Innocence of eye' is little else than this. . . . All that is asked

---

[1] *Scale of Perfection*, ii, 40.

is that we shall look for a little time, in a special and un-
divided manner, at some simple, concrete and external
thing. This object of our contemplation may be almost
anything we please: a picture, a statue, a tree, a distant hill-
side, a growing plant, running water, little living things.
We need not, with Kant, go to the starry heavens. 'A little
thing the quantity of an hazel nut' will do for us as it did
for Lady Julian long ago. Remember, it is a practical
experiment on which we are set; not an opportunity of
pretty and pantheistic meditation.

Look, then, at this thing which you have chosen. Wilfully
yet tranquilly refuse the messages which countless other
aspects of the world are sending; and so concentrate your
whole attention on this one act of loving sight that all other
objects are excluded from the conscious field. Do not think,
but, as it were, pour out your personality towards it: let
your soul be in your eyes. Almost at once, this new method
of perception will reveal unsuspected qualities in the
external world. First, you will perceive about you a strange
and deepening quietness; a slowing down of our feverish
mental time. Next, you will become aware of a heightened
significance, an intensified existence in the thing at which
you look. As you, with all your consciousness, lean out
towards it, an answering current will meet yours. It seems
as though the barrier between its life and your own,
between subject and object, had melted away. You are
merged with it in an act of true communion: and you *know*
the secret of its being deeply and unforgettably, yet in a way
which you can never hope to express.

Seen thus, a thistle has celestial qualities: a speckled hen
a touch of the sublime. Our greater comrades, the trees,
the clouds, the rivers initiate us into mighty secrets, flame
out at us 'like shining from shook foil.' The 'eye which

looks upon Eternity' has been given its opportunity. We have been immersed for a moment in the 'life of the All': a deep and peaceful love unites us with the substance of all things, a 'Mystic Marriage' has taken place between the mind and some aspect of the external world. *Cor ad cor loquitur*: Life has spoken to life, but not to the surface intelligence. That surface intelligence knows only that the message was beautiful: no more.

The price of this experience has been a stilling of that surface mind, a calling-in of all our scattered interests: an entire giving of ourselves to this one activity, without self-consciousness, without reflective thought. . . . The contemplative, on whatever level his faculty may operate, is contented to absorb and be absorbed: and by this humble access he attains to a plane of knowledge which no intellectual process can come near.

I do not suggest that this simple experiment is in any sense to be equated with the transcendental contemplation of the mystic. Yet it exercises on a small scale, and in regard to visible Nature, the same natural faculties which are taken up and used—it is true upon other levels, and in subjection to the transcendental sense—in his apprehension of the invisible Real. Though it is one thing to see truthfully for an instant the flower in the crannied wall, another to be lifted up to the apprehension of 'eternal Truth, true Love and loved Eternity,' yet both according to their measure are functions of the inward eye, operating in the 'suspension of the mind.' . . .

The contemplation of Spirit . . . requires a deliberate refusal of the messages of the senses, an ingoing or intro-version of our faculties a 'journey towards the centre.' The Kingdom of God, they say, is within you: seek it then, in the most secret habitations of the soul.

THE DARK KNOWLEDGE OF GOD

The soul that has received the intimation of the true relation between its small perceptions and the universe of Spirit, has experienced once for all the essence of that purgation of the understanding which prepares the way of faith. For what matters here is that the mind shall become so quietly limpid, so clear of its own deceptive notions and discriminations, that it receives simply and humbly the subtle touch of God; 'understanding because it does not seek to understand,'—as we understand the mystery of the night. Then we realise that prayer only achieves depth and substance when it passes beyond and above our intelligence; and we know not what we do, because our action is engulfed in the mighty act of Spirit, and we are for the time being lost in the night of God.

BARE FAITH

There is no correspondence, no parity, between our most admirable notions and the Being of God; and we only begin to approach a certain obscure knowledge of His presence when we consent to abandon our arrogant attempts towards definition and understanding, become the meek recipients of His given lights, and the silent worshippers of His unfathomable Reality. Only by a movement of bare faith does the mind really draw near to Him.

BEYOND THOUGHT

In the preliminary act of gathering yourself together, and in those unremitting explorations through which you came to 'a knowing and a feeling of yourself as you are,' thought assuredly had its place. There the powers of analysis, criticism and deduction found work that they could do. But now it is the love and will—the feeling, the intent, the passionate desire—of the self, which shall govern your activities and make possible your success. Few would care to brave the horrors of a courtship conducted upon strictly intellectual lines: and contemplation is an act of love, the wooing, not the critical study, of the Divine Reality. It is an eager outpouring of ourselves towards a Somewhat Other for which we feel a passion of desire; a seeking, touching and tasting, not a considering and analysing, of the beautiful and true wherever found.

PSYCHOLOGY AND THE LIFE OF THE SPIRIT

The law of reversed effort . . . is valid on every level of life, and warns us against the error of making religion too grim and strenuous an affair. Certainly in all life of the spirit the will is active and must retain its conscious and steadfast orientation to God. Heroic activity and moral effort must form an integral part of full human experience. Yet it is clearly possible to make too much of the process of wrestling with evil. An attention chiefly and anxiously concentrated on the struggle with sins and weaknesses, instead of on the eternal sources of happiness and power, will offer the unconscious harmful suggestions of impotence and hence tend to frustration. The early ascetics, who made elaborate preparations for dealing with temptations, got as an inevitable result plenty of temptations with which to deal. A sounder method is taught by the mystics. 'When thoughts of sin press on thee,' says *The Cloud of Unknowing*, 'look over their shoulders seeking another thing, the which thing is God. . . .'

Give the contemplative faculty its chance, let it breathe

for at least a few moments of each day the spiritual atmosphere of faith, hope and love, and the spiritual life will at least in some measure, be realized by it.

A SIMPLE DIRECTION FOR CONTEMPLATION

(*to a correspondent*)

In spite of all the mystics have told us, we are in (this) working with an almost unknown tool. Try this way:

1. Put yourself into some position so easy and natural to you that you do not notice your body: and shut your eyes.

2. Represent to your mind, some phrase, truth, dogma, event, e.g. a phrase of the Paternoster or *Anima Christi*, the Passion, the Nativity are the sort of things I use. Something that occurs naturally. Now, do not think about it but keep it before you, turning it over as you might finger some precious possession.

3. Deliberately, and by an act of will, shut yourself off from your senses. Do not attend to touch or hearing: till the external world seems unreal and far away. Still holding on to your idea, turn your attention *inwards* (this is what Ruysbroeck means by introversion) and allow yourself to sink, as it were, downwards and downwards, into the profound silence and peace which is the essence of the meditative state. More you cannot do for yourself: if you get further, you will do so automatically as a consequence of the above practice. It is the 'shutting off of the senses' and what Boehme calls the 'stopping the wheel of the imagination and ceasing from self-thinking' that is hard at first. Anyhow do not try these things when you are tired— it is useless: and do not give up the form of prayer that comes naturally to you; and do not be disheartened if it seems at

first a barren and profitless performance. It is quite possible to obtain spiritual nourishment without being consciously aware of it.

Read *Holy Wisdom* by the Ven. Augustine Baker.

THE PRAYER OF SILENCE

Those who believe in prayer at all should make a practice of setting aside some time each day in which they deliberately turn from all vocal acts and petitions and, placing themselves in a meek and simple attitude, remain thus quietly and simply in the presence of God. At first the time should be short: for beginners five or ten minutes is enough. The attention must be trained gradually, for those accustomed to 'say' their prayers will find this new intercourse difficult, making in the early stages, great demands upon their patience and self-control. The idea that silent prayer is a form of religious laziness comes only from those who have never tried it. At first thoughts, wants and memories rush into the mind; sounds and images distract it. There is something very humiliating in the way in which meaningless interruptions capture the attention which we are trying to fix upon God. All these invitations to break the silence must be refused and the self brought back again and again to its poise of listening, of humble, hushed attentiveness. 'Prayer in itself is nought else but a devout intent directed unto God' says one old English mystic. Here is its centre; hence spring all its beauties and powers. It is not meant that the whole of prayer should consist in silent absorption. But if we will learn by practice the art of retreating to its quiet centre, we can come out from this into the different branches of prayerful activity which charity and penitence demand of us. In the silence we see our way to perpetual fresh acts of adoration and intercession, of penitence and

petition, which are then genuine expressions of our love
and need and have behind them the whole weight of a will
which is for the time being in union with the will of God.
They arise spontaneously from the deeps of the soul, for we
are giving the spirit opportunity of utterance, too often
checked by mechanical and conventional methods of prayer.
Then it is that the veil is sometimes lifted and Perfect Love
mysteriously interprets to us the puzzles of eternity. That
which we hear in the silence will be conditioned by our
purity of mind, humility and charity. Sometimes it remains
unbroken and we receive only the gift of spiritual rest.
But sooner or later, all, according to their measure gain
from it some assurance of divine companionship, some
fresh strength for dealing with circumstance. They find in
the deep hush which then surrounds them, that prayers
inspired by love and trust are sifted out from those inspired
by fear and self-will: for it is in the silence that we learn to
pray. It is then, too, that we draw nearest the souls of the
departed, are best able to help them and pray for them, to
feel the communion between their life and ours.

Finally, the prayer of silence has an active and social as
well as a religious and personal value. In it the soul feeds
upon God; draws new vitality from the source of all life.
The citizen who is so strengthened is worth more to the
State than the man whose roots do not strike deep into
eternity. His work is better, his judgment saner, his ability
to bear pain, trial, suspense is enormously enhanced.
Therefore, the cultivation of our spiritual faculties is at the
present time a patriotic duty, and each one who deliberately
makes a place in his life for it, is doing a service to the
common cause.

(d) INTERCESSION

UXBRIDGE ROAD

The Western Road goes streaming out to seek the cleanly wild,
It pours the city's dim desires towards the undefiled,
It sweeps betwixt the huddled homes about its eddies grown
To smear the little space between the city and the sown:
The torments of that seething tide who is there that can see?
There's one who walked with starry feet the western road by me!

He is the Drover of the soul; he leads the flock of men
All wistful on that weary track, and brings them back again.
The dreaming few, the slaving crew, the motley cast of life—
The wastrel and artificer, the harlot and the wife—
They may not rest, for ever pressed by one they cannot see:
The one who walked with starry feet the western road by me.

He drives them east, he drives them west, between the dark and
    light;
He pastures them in city pens, he leads them home at night,
The towery trams, the threaded trains, like shuttles to and fro
To weave the web of working days in ceaseless travel go.
How harsh the woof, how long the weft! who shall the fabric see?
The one who walked with starry feet the western road by me!

Throughout the living joyful year at lifeless tasks to strive,
And scarcely at the end to save gentility alive;
The villa plot to sow and reap, to act the villa lie,
Beset by villa fears to live, midst villa dreams to die;
Ah, who can know the weary woe? and who the splendour see?
The one who walked with starry feet the western road by me.

158

Behold! he lent me as we went the vision of the seer;
Behold! I saw the life of men, the life of God shine clear.
I saw the Spirit's hidden thrust; I saw the race fulfil
The spiral of its steep ascent, predestined of the Will
Yet not unled, but shepherded by one they may not see—
The one who walked with starry feet the western road by me.

In intercession as a whole we have the simplest example provided by the general religious life, of a vast principle which is yet largely unexplored by us. It is the principle, that man's emergent will and energy can join itself to, and work with, the supernatural forces for the accomplishment of the work of God: sometimes for this purpose even entering into successful conflict with the energies of the 'natural world.'

MAN'S CONTRIBUTION TO GOD'S REDEMPTIVE WORK

There is an intercessory prayer which seems to have no specified aim. It is poured out, an offering of love, in order that it may be used; and this is specially true of its more developed forms in the interior life of devoted souls. As spiritual writers say, its energies and sufferings may simply be 'given to God,' added to the total sacrificial action of the Church. It may then do a work which remains forever unknown to the praying soul; contributing to the good of the whole universe of spirits, the conquest of evil, the promotion of the Kingdom, the increased energy of holiness. Such general and sacrificial prayer has always formed part of the interior life of the saints; and it is an enduring strand in the corporate work of the Church. . . .

It was of this aspect of prayer that Cardinal Mercier spoke when he said in one of his pastorals: 'Through an ever closer adherence to the Holy Spirit in the sanctuary of your soul, you can, from within your home circle, the heart of your country, the boundary of your parish, overpass all earthly frontiers, and, intensify and extend the Kingdom

of Love.' As the rhythm of Christ's life went to and fro
between adoring prayer on the mountain and the manifestation of the Divine redeeming power in the world, so
those two movements should form the rhythm of the life
of prayer. For only such a double life can express our double
relation to Spirit; the entire dependence on that which is
higher than our highest and the faithful mediation of that
which is nearer than our most inward part.

CREATIVE ACTION

Real intercession is in the last resort a part of the creative
action of God, exercised through those created spirits
which have achieved a certain union with Him. And it
requires for its real and safe exercise that temper of humble
worship, and that habitude of docile correspondence, which
the life of adoration and communion develops in the soul.
Only a will that is purified and nourished by the indwelling
Spirit and confirmed in the humble knowledge of its own
dependent state, can recognize those quiet pressures which
indicate the path its intercessions should take, and subordinate its work for souls to the overruling Divine Will:
preserved from perverse desires and vagrant choices by its
meek and adoring inclination towards God.

THE COSTINGNESS OF INTERCESSION

The great intercessor must possess an extreme sensitive-
ness to the state and needs of souls and of the world. As
those who live very close to nature become tuned to her
rhythm, and can discern in solitary moments all the movements of her secret life, or as musicians distinguish each
separate note in a great symphony and yet receive the
music as a whole; so the intercessor, whether living in the

world or enclosed in a convent (for these are only differ-
ences in technique) is sensitized to every note and cadence
in the rich and intricate music of common life. He stretches
out over an ever wider area the filaments of love, and
receives and endures in his own person the anguish of its
sorrow, its helplessness, its confusions, and its sin; suffering
again and again the darkness of Gethsemane and the Cross,
as the price of his redemptive power. For it is his awful
privilege to stand in the gap between the world's infinite
need and the treasuries of the Divine Love.

THE SELFLESSNESS OF CHRISTIAN PRAYER

The whole rich tangle of creation, loved and supported
by God, must be the concern of all who are given to God.
He is as fully and intimately present with the tomtit as with
the Milky Way; He 'sails with those who are sailing, travels
with the wayfarers in the way, and is Physician both of body
and of soul.' There is no human situation or human need
which lies outside the radius of the Divine Compassion and
cannot be the material of our intercessory care.

So the Christian communicant must become ever more
sensitive to the pressure of this creative love, driving us to all
possible objects of love, small as well as great. Those whose
lives are self-offered on the Altar of Holy Desire, are
transferred once for all from the sphere of private enterprise
to that of co-operative action.

Only as a cell of the Body of Christ, a capacity for the
Spirit, an agent of the supernatural action, can the individual
intercede. It comes to offer the sacrifice, yet is itself part
of the sacrifice. The Eucharistic life is not a devotional
addition to existence but the clue to all real existence whether
social or personal. It is concerned with the mighty realities
of evil and redemption, death and life. The more deeply

the soul enters into the great movement of the Liturgy, the more this truth is experienced; and all devotional pettiness, all spiritual self-seeking purged away.

CO-OPERATION WITH GOD

Physical and mental labour, no less than spiritual labour, can become the vehicles of spiritual effectiveness: for the worth of intercession abides, not in the specific things which it can and does do for man, but in the unimpeded channel offered by its loving intention to the transforming Divine love and will. There is included in its work that strange power of one spirit to penetrate, illuminate, support and rescue other spirits, through which so much of the spiritual work of the world seems to be done; the more awful privilege of redemptive suffering, as it appears again and again in the lives of the saints; the total dedication of the contemplative, redressing in adoration the downward trend of our largely self-interested world; the strong out-streaming prayer of the cloistered nun, given for the general need. Not only these, but the scientist's costly battle with disease; the heroic reformer's struggle for social purity; the joyful endurance of physical pain and weakness which makes many a sick-bed into a radiant centre of spiritual power. By each such act and life the tiny human creature, if only for a moment, contributes to that spiritualizing of the natural order which 'takes away the sin of the world.'

V

SANCTIFICATION, THE GROWTH IN LOVE

CONTINUOUS VOYAGE[1]

At twilight, when I lean the gunwale o'er
And watch the water turning from the bow,
I sometimes think that best is here and now—
The voyage all, and nought the hidden shore.
Is there no help? and must we make the land?
Shall every sailing in some haven cease?
And must the chain run out, the anchor strike the sand,
And is there from its fetters no release?
And shall the Steersman's voice say, 'Nevermore
The ravening gale, the soft and sullen fog,
No more the cunning shoal, the changeful ebb and flow.
Put up the charts, and take the lead below,
And close the vessel's log'?

Adventure is a seaman's life, the port
Calls but the weary and the tempest driven:
Perhaps its safety were too dearly bought
If that for this our freedom must be given.
For lo! our Steersman is for ever young
And with much gladness sails beneath the stars;
Our ship is old, yet still her sails are hung
Like eager wings upon the steady spars.
Then tell me not of havens for the soul
Where tides can never come, nor storms molest;
My sailing spirit seeks no sheltered goal,
Nought is more sad then safety—life is best
When every day brings danger for delight,
And each new solemn night
Engulfs our whitening wake within the whole.

[1] Probably written at sea as she sailed every summer in her father's yacht: these thoughts no doubt came to her during her 'trick' at the helm.

Beyond the bent horizon oceans are
Where every star
Lies like an isle upon Eternity.
There would I be
Given to his rushing wind,
No prudent course to find
For some snug corner of Infinity;
But evermore to sail
Close-reefed before the gale,
And see the steep
Great billow of his love, with threatening foam,
Come roaring home
And lift my counter in its mighty sweep.

HIDDEN GROWTH

ALL gardeners know the importance of good root development before we force the leaves and flowers. So our life in God should be deeply rooted and grounded before we presume to expect to produce flowers or fruits; otherwise we risk shooting up into one of those lanky plants which never do without a stick. We are constantly beset by the notion that we ought to perceive ourselves springing up quickly, like the seed on stony ground; showing striking signs of spiritual growth. But perhaps we are only required to go on quietly, making root, growing nice and bushy, docile to the great slow rhythm of life. When we see no startling marks of our own religious progress or our usefulness to God, it is well to remember the baby in the stable and the little boy in the streets of Nazareth. The very life was there present which was to change the whole history of the human race; the rescuing action of God. At that stage there was not much to show for it; yet there is perfect continuity between the stable and the Easter Garden, and the thread that unites them is the hidden Will of God. The childish prayer of Nazareth was the right preparation for the awful prayer of the Cross.

So it is that the life of the Spirit is to unfold gently and steadily within us; till at last the full stature for which God designed us, is attained.

GROWTH AND TRANSFORMATION

Every human soul without exception, because of its mysterious affinity with God, and yet its imperfect

169

status, its unlikeness from God, is called to undertake a growth and a transformation which shall make of it a channel of the Divine energy and will. Such a statement as this is not to be narrowed down and limited to that which we call the 'religious' life. On the contrary it affirms the religious character of all full life. For it means a kind of self-oblivious faithfulness in response to all the various demands of circumstance, the carrying through of everything to which one sets one's hand, which is rooted in a deep loyalty to the interests of God. That conception expands our idea of the religious life far beyond the devotional life, till there is room in it for all the multiple activities of man in so far as they are prosecuted in, for, and with the Fact of all facts, God-Reality. I need not point out that for Christians the Incarnation and its extension in the Church bring together these two movements in the soul and in the human complex; and start a vast process to which every awakened soul which rises above self-interest, has some contribution to make. As we become spiritually sensitive and more alert in our response to experience, I think we sometimes get a glimpse of that deep creative action by which we are being brought into this new order of being, more and more transformed into the agents of spirit; able to play our part in the great human undertaking of bringing the whole world nearer to the intention of God. We then perceive the friction of circumstance, the hard and soft of life, personal contacts and opportunities, love and pain and dreariness, to be penetrated and used by a Living Influence, which is making by this means both changes and positive additions to our human nature; softening, deepening, enriching and moulding the raw material of temperament into something nearer the artist's design.

PATIENCE WITH OURSELVES

Only the Peace of God, a constant turning in our prayers to His abiding tranquillity is going to . . . make us realize that patience with ourselves is a duty for Christians and the only real humility. For it means patience with a growing creature whom God has taken in hand and whose completion He will effect in His own time and His own way. *Rest in the Lord, wait patiently on Him and He shall give thee thy heart's desire.* The more central this thought becomes the less difficult you will find its outward expression; that is to say, long-suffering and gentleness in all the encounters of everyday life. . . .

It is God Who gives the conditions. Our part is to accept them with humility and cultivate the quiet spirit of acceptance; to adjust our will to His great rhythm and not waste the strength He has given us fighting against the stream.

In the midst of the waters I shall be with thee.

THE SANCTIFYING OF PERSONALITY

Sanctification means the universalizing of the creature's will and love; their dedication to the interests of Reality. Thus, if the prayer of adoration and communion brings man to an ever deeper consciousness of his own faulty nature—obliges him to work with God in the supernaturalizing of his own selfhood by the secret labours of self-conquest—this call to purgation of character is only the first point in the real sanctifying of personality. Sooner or later he will realize that this reformation is being effected for a purpose; in order that he may co-operate in the workings of the Supernatural on and in other souls.

CRUCIFIXION OF SELF-INTEREST

Every heroic devotion to beauty, truth, goodness, every ungrudging sacrifice, is a crucifixion of self-interest, and thus lies in the direction of sanctity; and wherever we find sanctity we find the transforming act of God, of super-nature, upon the creature, irrespective of that creature's dogmatic belief. All Saints, that 'glorious touching Company' will doubtless include many whom the world classed among its irreligious men.

THE INSTRUMENTS OF SANCTITY

There is no parity whatever between the intensity of those external, or even internal, trials which discipline us, and their purifying result. The dripping tap or barking dog which teaches patience is as much an instrument of God as the shattering blow which tears two souls apart. A soul in the sphere of purification may receive the maximum of suffering—and, if abandoned to God, the maximum of cleansing—through an apparently inadequate event; if the response which that event demands be of such a nature as to mortify the root of self-regard. Even the outward incidents of the Passion were not proportioned to the dread suffering and victory of which they were the proximate cause. One and the same event may be charged for this soul with the purifying call to an utter self-abandonment; and merely incite that soul to a sterile resentment. The cleansing and transforming power of suffering abides not in the degree of pain experienced, but in the degree of acceptance achieved; the *Fiat voluntas tua* with which the soul meets the action of God-Spirit in and through events.

CREATIVE SPIRITUAL LIFE

Dante says that directly a soul ceases to say *Mine* and says *Ours*, it makes the transition from the narrow, constricted individual life to the truly free, truly personal, truly creative spiritual life in which all are linked together in one single response to the Father of all spirits, God. Here all interpenetrate, and all, however humble and obscure their lives may seem, can and do affect each other. Every advance made by one is made for all.

Only when we recognize this and act on it are we fully alive and taking our proper place in the universe of spirits; for life means the fullest possible give and take between the living creature and its environment. And spiritual life, which is profoundly organic, means the give and take, the willed correspondence of the little human spirit with the Infinite Spirit, here where it is; its feeding upon Him, its growth towards perfect union with Him, its response to His attraction and subtle pressure. . . .

There are countless ways in which this may happen: sometimes under conditions which seem to the world like the very frustration of life, of progress, of growth. Thus boundless initiative is chained to a sick-bed and transmuted into sacrifice; the lover of beauty is sent to serve in the slum; the lover of stillness is kept on the run all day, the sudden demand to leave all comes to the one who least expects it, and through and in these apparent frustrations the life of the spirit emerges and grows. So those who imagine they are called to contemplation because they are attracted by contemplation, when the common duties of existence steadily block this path, do well to realize that our own feelings and preferences are very poor guides when it comes to the robust realities and stern demands of the Spirit.

SUFFERING AND SANCTITY

Since there is for man no tension and no problem when God's Will and human preference happen to agree, and in fact the drive and demand of the Will is then hardly perceived by us, it follows that it is most often in suffering, willed and accepted, that the real transcendence of egoism is accomplished. This does not mean that suffering is in itself holy; but that, being what we are, it nearly always accompanies our full acceptance of the Holy and its tremendous demands.

And, last, the Will is to be done 'as in Heaven'; peacefully, joyfully, perfectly, the response of a deep and disciplined love.

THE IMPROBABLE PATH OF SANCTITY

A strange reversal of fortune, the frustration of obviously excellent plans, lies behind most of the triumphs of Christian history. It was by an unlikely route that Christ Himself, the country carpenter, itinerant preacher, and victim of local politics, carried humanity up into God. It was in defiance alike of the probable and the suitable that St. Paul was chosen, seized, transmuted, and turned to the purposes of the Will. Stephen, full of grace and power, is snatched in the splendour of his faith to God; and His Will is achieved and the Catholic Church is created by the abrupt conversion of a brilliant young scholar to a small revivalist sect. If we think of St. Paul's situation at the opening of his apostolic life—the humiliating eating of his own words, the long-lived suspicion and unpopularity, and his constancy through it all—it becomes clear that only the immense pressure of God's Will, overwhelming all natural reluctances and desires, can account for it. Nor did the rest of St. Paul's life, mostly spent in exhausting, dangerous and often disappointing labours, contain much food for ambition or self-love. Christian history looks glorious in retrospect; but it is made up of constant hard choices and unattractive tasks, accepted under the pressure of the Will.

In the volume of the book it is written of me, that I should fulfil Thy Will, O my God: I am content to do it.

ORDINARY LIFE AND ITS EXTRAORDINARY PURPOSE

'Though I give my body to be burned,' said St. Paul, 'and have not love, I am nothing.' I do not as a supernatural being exist. And now he gives us another and much more surprising test of spiritual vitality. Though you feel an unconquerable love, joy and peace, though you are gentle, long-suffering, good in all your personal relationships, though you are utterly faithful in your service of God—in the end the only proof that all this is truly fruit of the Spirit, Christ in you and not just your own idea, is the presence of the last two berries on the bunch: not showy berries, not prominently placed, but absolutely decisive for classification of the plant. Meekness and Temperance says the Authorized Version or, as we may quite properly translate, Humility and Moderation. That means our possession of the crowning grace of creatureliness: knowing our own size and own place, the self-oblivion and quietness with which we fit into God's great scheme instead of having a jolly little scheme of our own, and are content to bring forth the fruit of His Spirit, according to our own measure, here and now in space and time.

Humility and Moderation—the graces of the self-forgetful soul—we might almost expect that, if we have grasped all that the Incarnation really means—God and His love manifest not in some peculiar and supernatural spiritual manner, but in ordinary human nature. Christ, first-born of many brethren, content to be one of us, living the family life, and from within His Church inviting the souls of men to share the family life . . . How right St. Paul was to put these two fruits at the end of his list, for as a rule they are the very last we acquire. At first we simply do not see the point. But the saints have always seen it. When Angela of Foligno was dying her disciples asked for a last message and she, who had been called a Mistress in Theology and whose Visions of the Being of God are among the greatest the medieval mystics have left us, had only one thing to say to them as her farewell: 'Make yourselves small! Make yourselves very small!'

LOVE IN SELF-DONATION

The final cleansing of the will and heart requires the soul to disregard her own inevitable alternations of pain and pleasure, communion and dereliction; to escape from introspection and subjectivity into the bracing atmosphere of God. She is to lose herself in the great Divine purpose, and in His will find her unbreakable peace. For though this final transforming action of Spirit on the soul is first experienced as a purifying inward suffering, while our conscious disharmony with God persists; when the soul has at last become pliant to Him and His interests, it enters into a very quiet and unanalysed condition of freedom and joy.

The saints have ever sought with an increasing ardour this simple and self-oblivious idea. As faith and hope more utterly possessed them and subdued to one purpose all the powers of the soul, so an entire and loving self-donation in and through circumstance has seemed to them to contain within itself the whole substance of a spiritual life. 'What require I more of thee, than that thou shouldst study wholly

to resign thyself to me?' Indeed it is the beggar-maid's only
possible response to Cophetua: for all that she has is her will
and her love.

RECONSTRUCTION OF PERSONALITY

'Man,' says Boehme, 'must here be at war with himself
if he wishes to be a heavenly citizen . . . fighting must be
the watchword, not with tongue and sword, but with
mind and spirit—and not to give over.'

The need of such a conflict, shown to us in history, is
explained on human levels by psychology. On spiritual
levels it is made plain to all whose hearts are touched by the
love of God. By this way all must pass who achieve the
life of the Spirit; subduing to its purposes their wayward
wills and sublimating in its power their conflicting animal
impulses. This long effort brings as its reward a unification
of character, an inflow of power: from it we see the mature
man or woman of the spirit emerge . . . The ending of this
conflict, the self's unification and establishment in the new
life, commonly means a return more or less complete to
that world from which the convert had retreated; a taking
up of the fully energized and fully consecrated human
existence which must express itself in work no less than in
prayer, an exhibition, too, of the capacity for leadership
which is the mark of the regenerate mind. . . . On the
highest levels of the spiritual life . . . this experience and
realization; first, of profound harmony with Eternity and
its interests; next, of a personal relation of love; last, of an
indwelling creative power, a givenness, an energizing grace,
reaches that completeness to which has been given the
name of union with God.

The great man or woman of the Spirit who achieves this
perfect development is, it is true, a special product: a genius

comparable with great creative personalities in other walks of life . . . Like other artists he founds a school; the spiritual life *flames* up and spreads to those within his circle of influence. Through him ordinary men, whose aptitude for God might have remained latent, obtain a fresh start. . . . There is a sense in which he might say with the Johannine Christ, 'He that receiveth me receiveth Him that sent me . . .'

THE WILL

Will is character in action; and sanctity, which is simply character transformed upon supernatural levels, means above all else the complete and unreserved collaboration of this energetic will with the active grace of God.

TRANSCENDENCE

Faith, Hope and Charity—to give these states of soul their traditional names—remain the essential conditions under which man can transcend himself; the dispositions in which alone he can bear the stresses and make the sacrifices which are involved in every increase in his knowledge of Reality. Not anxious conflicts, but a self-forgetting and all-enduring enthusiasm best draw him on; whether his assigned end be that of the discoverer, the artist or the saint.

VI

PENITENCE, THE OUTCOME OF LOVE

APOCALYPSE

'I saw,' said John the Seer,
'New Heaven and new earth.' But I, each day,
Behold thy new creation that draws near
On every budding spray.
Yea, down the stream of time the thundering hoofs I hear
Of horses shining white and strangely grey,
That bear upon their way
The kings of death and life, the true and faithful kings.

'I saw,' said John the Seer,
'The Mother of all life, her travailings.'
But I have seen the birth of many a year,
And lovely childish things
Snatched back to God because they are so dear
No haven can avail, save his enshrouding wings.
I've known the sudden palms of many springs
Pass, like a fleeting sacrament of grace.

'I saw,' said John the Seer,
'The Ever-Living One, his awful face.'
I in pools deep and clear
Have plunged my look to trace
Faint and austere
In some uncharted place
Secure from flitting time, released from narrow space,
The First and Last, the Beauty new and old.

'I saw,' said John the Seer,
'The dreadful judgements of his wrath unfold.'
I am not thus. I know not how to fear
That love which drew the crocus from the mould:

181

Nor, whilst the skylark's song is in mine ear,
Can hear a sterner voice than that which told
His vengeful hosts their fury to withhold
From green things, grass and trees,
Lest hurt should fall on these;
And said, that when his heaven indeed was come,
With men his tent should be, with men his wandering home,.
And God should heal their griefs, and wipe away each tear.

By false desires and false thoughts man has built up for himself a false universe; as a mollusc by the deliberate absorption of lime and rejection of all else, can build up for itself a hard shell which shuts it from the external world, and only represents in a distorted and unrecognizable form, the ocean from which it was obtained. This hard shell, this one-sided secretion of the surface consciousness, makes as it were a little cave of illusion for each separate soul. A literal and deliberate getting out of the cave must be for every mystic, as it was for Plato's prisoners, the first step in the individual hunt for reality.

That world which we have distorted by identifying it with our own self-regarding arrangements of its elements, has got to reassume for us the character of Reality, of God. In the purified sight of the great mystics it did reassume this character; their shells were opened wide, they knew the tides of the Eternal Sea. This lucid apprehension of the True is what we mean when we speak of the Illumination which results from a faithful acceptance of the trials of the Purgative Way.

That which we call the 'natural' self as it exists in the 'natural' world—the 'old Adam' of St. Paul—is wholly incapable of supersensual adventure. All its activities are grouped about a centre of consciousness whose correspondences are with the material world. In the moment of its awakening, it is abruptly made aware of this disability. It knows itself finite. It now aspires to the Infinite. It is encased in the hard crust of individuality; it aspires to union with a larger self. It is fettered; it longs for freedom. . . .

Though the end of mysticism is not adequately defined as goodness, it entails the acquirement of goodness. The virtues are the 'ornaments of the Spiritual Marriage' because that marriage is union with the Good no less than with the Beautiful and the True.

Primarily then, the self must be purged of all that stands between it and goodness: putting on the character of reality instead of the character of illusion or 'sin.' It longs ardently to do this from the first moment in which it sees itself in the all-revealing radiance of the Uncreated Light. 'When Love openeth the eyes of the soul to see this truth,' says Hilton, 'then beginneth the soul forsooth to be vastly meek. For then by the sight of God it feeleth and seeth itself as it is and then doth the soul forsake the beholding and leaning to itself.' (*Scale of Perfection*, II. 37.)

So with Dante, the first terrace of the Mount of Purgatory is devoted to the cleansing of pride and the production of humility, the inevitable result of a vision, however fleeting, of Reality and an undistorted sight of the earthbound self. All its life that self has been measuring its candlelight by other candles. Now for the first time it is out in the open air and sees the sun. 'This is the way,' said the voice of God to St. Catherine of Siena in ecstasy: 'If thou wilt arrive at a perfect knowledge and enjoyment of Me, the Eternal Truth, thou shouldst never go outside the knowledge of thyself; and by humbling thyself in the valley of humility thou wilt know Me and thyself, from which knowledge thou wilt draw all that is necessary. . . . In self-knowledge then, thou wilt humble thyself; seeing that in thyself thou dost not even exist' . . .

To the true lover of the Absolute, Purgation no less than Illumination is a privilege, a dreadful joy. It is an earnest of increasing life.

CONTRITION AND RESPONSE

When we recognize the gentle touch of the Holy and the Perfect on our smudged imperfect selves, then contrition, because our response is so impaired by slackness, self-indulgence and sin, overwhelms and humbles us. And in so doing it opens our souls to the purifying action of Spirit, softens and tranquillizes and increases our capacity for God. 'How delicately thou teachest love to me!' says St. John of the Cross. If we are ever to learn it, we must be ready to move with suppleness between the most unearthly and most personal recognitions. We must recognize our own poverty over against the generous Divine richness; our own guilt in respect of the crucifixion of Divine Love. We must by turns ascend to the spire-top of the spirit, and sink into the deeps of the soul's ground. For all the resources of poetry and all the contrasting images and experiences of man's emotional life, can only suggest but never give the content of this simple yet incredible intercourse between the fugitive in its weakness and instability, and the Abiding in its infinite power.

SIN, SORROW AND JOY

Because of 'sin,' because of that strange element within the world which opposes God, and perverts His gifts, all . . . working of the Supernatural in human life must involve suffering and tension. Real temptation, struggle, darkness, is involved in every genuine transcendence of the 'natural man.' Yet since this transcendence is the very condition of the fulfilment of personality, it brings even through effort a real and vivid joy, an ever-deepening peace and harmony, to the soul that undertakes it.

SELF-SCRUTINY

The Christian cannot elude ethics on his way to the sanctuary of God. Over against the contrite acknowledgement of our own faultiness, our ingrained egotism and turbulent desires, the Church sets the acknowledgement of our responsibility, and the bracing appeal to the moral will. Humility does not mean an easy acquiescence in our own shabbiness. The human nature which is to be offered at the altar for God's purpose, must be ordered and purified, in so far as man is able to do it. He must at least set his life in order as well as he can, submit thought, word and deed to the judgement of Love before he goes further. 'Let a man examine himself,' says St. Paul to those who come to the Christian mysteries. Not as to whether he is good enough, for this question is not worth asking; but as to whether he is willing to take trouble enough, whether his face is set towards Eternity, and whether the demands and interests of the Eternal are given priority over the demands and interests of self-will. Self-conquest in its most realistic and costly form is asked of the Christian communicant. A purely mystical religion, leaving the sense-world and its conflicts behind in its flight towards God, might elude all this; but an incarnational religion never can. It must unify and carry forward humanity in its wholeness, in its approach to the altar of God.

THE LOVE THAT BURNS TO HEAL

Were the mere escape from consequence, the blotting-out of transgressions, the object of our prayer, how greatly it would fall beneath the level on which Christ has placed man's relation to God; and how easy a concession it would offer to our inveterate self-love. Instead of an easy concession, the Divine forgiveness makes a heroic demand upon our courage. For that forgiveness is not the easy passing of a sponge over a slate. It is a stern and painful process: it means the re-ordering of the soul's disordered love, setting right what is wrong, washing it from wickedness and cleansing it from sin. Theology declares that original sin, disturbing the balance and harmony of man's nature, causes especially four kinds of spiritual damage: ignorance, malice, weakness and claimful desire. Here are the roots of our worst de-ordinations; and these the Charity of God must cure. That Charity must compel self-knowledge, kill animosity, brace the will and mortify desire. Playing without hindrance on the soul that craves for forgiveness it burns to heal; redeems, transforms and purifies all at once. The Lord's Prayer contains no direct demand for purification because pardon, the restoration of a loving relation with the Perfect, involves purification. The penitent soul accepts the jurisdiction of Charity, and Charity will have its perfect and searching work; burning up the chaff in the unquenchable fire of love. The cleansing pains of contrition are part of the mercy of God.

'FORGIVE US OUR TRESPASSES'

A whole type of prayer, a special and intimate relation with the Unseen, brought into existence by the very fact of our mixed half-animal nature, the ceaseless tension between the pull of earth and the demand of heaven, is summed up in these four words.

The sequence of Antiphons which the ancient Church ordained for the opening days of Lent—a liturgical direction, as it were, for the intention of the penitent Christian soul— shows how many-sided is our creaturely need for the pitying indulgence and redeeming action of God. 'Lord, that I may have light. . . . Wash me thoroughly from wickedness, and cleanse me from sin. . . . Lord, my servant lieth sick of the palsy. . . . Lord, I am not worthy that thou shouldst come under my roof: but say the word only and my soul shall be healed.'

Each phrase casts its searchlight on our condition. We need light, for the eyes of the mind are darkened, so that we cannot see the reality of our state; we need cleansing, for our very selfhood is sullied and impure. Our souls are sick and helpless, for sin has sapped their energy; we need a new dower of vitality from beyond ourselves if we are to become the sons of the Kingdom and serve the creative purpose of the Will. We end with an act of total and contrite confidence in God's restoring action—the crown of penitence: 'Say the word only, and my soul shall be healed.'

THE PLEA OF PENITENCE

'*We* are not worthy so much as to gather up the crumbs under Thy table,' says the English Prayer of Humble Access, with its reminiscence of the Phoenician woman pleading for her child: 'Yea, Lord! But the little dogs—the puppies—gather up the crumbs under the table!' Here, the soul does not even claim that privilege. It will not ask so much as the puppies' place; but puts the whole stress on the unmerited Divine generosity, the mysterious outpouring of creative love. *Domine, non sum dignus.*

My claim is so urgent, because my rights are non-existent and my need is so great. . . .

THE PRICE OF PEACE

O Lamb of God, that takest away the sins of the world, grant us Thy peace! That is a tremendous prayer to take on our

lips, for it means peace at a great price; the peace of the
Cross, of absolute acceptance, utter abandonment to God—
a peace inseparable from sacrifice. The peace-offering was
one of the three great Temple sacrifices and the one in
which the offerer drew nearest to God and had communion with God.

SELF-IMPROVEMENT AND SELF-SURRENDER

Let us look into our minds and souls. Could we claim a
clean bill of health? Is our whole psychical and spiritual
machinery running right, quite adjusted and adequate to
circumstances? No old wounds to self-esteem that give us
twinges? No auto-intoxication of jealous resentment,
depression quietly going on? No acidity? No displace-
ments, adhesions, no chronic ailments? Are we fit, as His
agents should be, for all weathers, all jobs? 'Try me,
O God, and seek the ground of my heart' says the Psalmist:
'Look well if there be any way of wickedness in me and
lead me in the way everlasting.' That kind of internal
examination may be very painful, very shaming, searching;
but only those willing to submit to it can hope for the full
healing of Christ. His diagnosis comes before His treatment.
All sin is disease . . . We can't produce the right anti-toxin
ourselves. He must enter our lives with His spirit of humility
and renunciation and cleanse us of infection . . . Somehow,
we don't know how, He gives us release. . . .

The self-abandoned prayer which ceases its own struggles
and its own patent medicines and places itself with entire
confidence in His hand, alone opens up paths for His healing
energy. 'Lord! if Thou wilt Thou canst. Say the word
only. I know you can say it. Have mercy! Cast forth my
particular devil. I can't!'

So too, if we hand ourselves over with confidence and

without reserve He will exercise on us His preventive medicine, simplify our lives, teach us what to do and what to leave out, persuade us to a plainer, more wholesome spiritual diet.

SELF-EMANCIPATION

There is a marvellous moment at the end of the *Purgatorio*, in which a tremor passes through the Holy Mountain; and all the souls on all the terraces, forgetting their own pains, rise to their feet in joy and sing the Gloria. And when Dante asks what has happened, he is told that one soul, casting off the last fetters of selfish desire, has risen and gone forward in freedom to God. In that one act, which turns the whole of the self's will towards the Universal Will, purification is complete. But so tough are the attachments of the senses, so inveterate is the creature's frenzied clutch on fugitive possessions and delights, that many minor operations are necessary before all the adhesions are cleared away.

FORGIVENESS AND FORTH-GIVING-NESS

There is nothing more purifying, more redeeming than the penitent love which is awakened by the generous forgiveness of another love. It opens a door in the brick wall which self-esteem has built between itself and God. But hardness, unpitying resentment, are the gates of hell. There shall be weeping and gnashing of teeth: the helpless misery of the angry egoist.

There are two perennial situations in which the human creature, whether individually or as a group, has to exercise that self-oblivious charity which is the essence of forgiveness. First, the cases in which it considers that its established rights have been infringed—trespasses: where the vigorous self-love of others has threatened its national, social, professional or emotional claims. Secondly, the cases in which it considers that its own just demands on affection, deference, consideration, possessions or status, have not been met—debts. Either by attack or by neglect, singly or as a body, the creature's self-love, its fundamental pride, is injured; and its anger aroused.

VII

DISCIPLINE, THE TRAINING IN LOVE

HEAVEN OR HELL

'. . . Ubi nos omnes unus amoris ignis sumus, qui major est,
quam quaeunque unquam condita sunt a Deo.'—RUYSBROECK

Let me whilst yet I can,
In this life's span,
Stretch to the Only Fair,
And teach my homing heart to breathe its native air.
Let me, whilst yet I may,
Learn to endure
Love's living flame most pure;
Its anguish that is joy,
Its piercing light
That must destroy
My night
And merge my moment in the Eternal Day.

In no celestial place,
Of no seraphic race,
Shall I acquire that art of blessedness;
But of my playmates in life's littleness,
My comrades in life's care.
Ah! let me not from that long schooling turn:
Lest when I wake,
Death's heritage of mystery to take,
My dimmed and frosted spirit may not bear
Upon that Hearth to burn,
Within that Light to dwell,
And so God's flaming heart become my Hell.

MANY people seem to think that the spiritual life necessarily requires a definite and exacting plan of study. It does not. But it does require a definite plan of life and courage in sticking to the plan, not merely for days or weeks, but for years. New mental and emotional habits must be formed, all our interests rearranged in new proportion round a new centre. This is something which cannot be hurried; but, unless we take it seriously, can be infinitely delayed. Many people suggest by their behaviour that God is of far less importance than their bath or morning paper, or early cup of tea. The life of co-operation with Him must begin with a full and practical acceptance of the truth that God alone matters—and that He, the Perfect, always desires perfection. Then it will inevitably press us to begin working for perfection; first, in our own characters and actions; next, in our homes, surroundings, profession and country. We must be prepared for the fact that even on small and personal levels this will cost a good deal; frequently thwarting our own inclinations and demanding real sacrifice.

TRANSFORMATION OF THE WILL

The cleansing, bracing and transforming of the will and emotional life is the hardest and most searching of all the soul's purifications. For it requires us to take the Cross into the most hidden sanctuary of personality, and complete that living sacrifice which the mortifying of the senses began. Now we must be ready not merely to renounce natural self-fulfilment and consolation, but super-natural self-fulfilment and consolation too; placing ourselves without reserve in the hand of God, and subordinating our small interests to the deep requirements of His mysterious life. As human love only achieves nobility when Eros is converted into Agape, when crude desire is sublimated, and becomes a self-giving tenderness; so with the craving for God which possesses all awakened souls. Only in so far as it compels us to a single undemanding act of self-giving can it be reckoned as purged of self-love; and only this simple and unconditioned charity can make of the soul a point of insertion for the action of the Spirit within the human world—a tool of the Divine creative will. . . .

THE NEW SELF

By mortification . . . is to be understood the positive aspect of purification: the remaking in relation to reality of the permanent elements of character. These elements, so far, have subserved the interests of the old self, worked for it in the world of sense. Now they must be adjusted to the needs of the new self and to the transcendent world in which it moves. Their focal point is the old self, the lower centre of consciousness; and the object of mortification is to kill that old self, remove that lower centre, in order that the higher centre, the 'new man,' may live and breathe. As St. Teresa discovered when she tried to reconcile the claims of friendship and contemplation, one or other must go: a house divided against itself cannot stand. 'Who hinders thee more,' says Thomas à Kempis, 'than the unmortified affections of thy own heart? . . . If we were perfectly dead unto ourselves and not entangled within our own breasts, then we should be able to taste Divine things and to have some experience of heavenly contemplation' . . . Real detachment means the death of preferences of all kinds: even of those which seem to other men the very proofs of virtue and fine taste.

SELF-STRIPPING

All pouring out of will and desire towards lesser objects, unless Spirit remains the ultimate aim, breaks up the unity of the soul's life and wastes its powers. This stern truth, indeed, rules all levels of our existence; and requires of us the normal restraints of common sense, as well as the absolute self-stripping of sanctity.

PURIFICATION

We are apt to think of 'mortification' as a codified moral discipline, imposed from without on the soul; whereas it really arises from the very character of the spiritual life, and is above all an evidence of growth. It is the name of those inevitable changes which the psyche must undergo, in the transfer of interest from self to God. Active purification represents the simple effort of our embryonic faith, hope and charity—three aspects and expressions of one state or tendency to God, as realized by the understanding will and heart—to capture and rule the house of the soul, and vanquish all hostile powers. Passive purification is best understood as a part of the Spirit's general creative action on us; given through circumstances and interior movements, and felt specially in the pressure of His demands on our innate self-will and self-love. 'It is one and the same flame of love,' says St. John of the Cross, 'which will one day unite itself to the soul to glorify it, and which now invades it to purify it.'

SACRIFICE, THE EXPRESSION OF LOVE

The awakened soul must often suffer perplexity, share to the utmost the stress and anguish of the physical order; and, chained as it is to a consciousness accustomed to respond to that order, must still be content with flashes of understanding, and willing to bear long periods of destitution when the light is veiled.

The further it advances the more bitter will these periods of destitution seem to it. It is not from the real men and women of the Spirit that we hear soft things about the comfort of faith. For the true life of faith gives everything worth having and takes everything worth offering: with unrelenting blows it welds the self into the stuff of the universe, subduing it to the universal purpose, doing away with the flame of separation. Though joy and inward peace, even in desolation, are dominant marks of those who have grown up into it, still it offers to none a succession of supersensual delights.

The life of the Spirit involves the sublimation of that pleasure-pain rhythm which is characteristic of normal consciousness, and if for it pleasure becomes joy, pain becomes the Cross. Toil, abnegation, sacrifice are therefore of its essence; but these are not felt as a heavy burden, because they are the expression of love.

SPIRITUAL WARFARE

The maturing of our personality, its full transformation in God, could hardly be achieved unless we were left in an apparent independence; to suffer, accept, deal with circumstances as real incarnate spirits, subject to all the vicissitudes of physical life. Our courage and loyalty must be tested by a genuine experience of solitude and darkness, if all our latent possibilities are to be realized.

'O Lord, your battles *do* last a long time !' said poor Suso, worn out by the disciplines, sufferings and reverses through which his ardent but unsteady soul was brought into stability and peace. Certainly life is not made soft for Christians, though it is in the last resort made safe. Nor do the struggles of the spiritual life—even the most crucial and most heroic—either look or feel very glorious while they are going on. Muddy trenches, great watchfulness and weariness, a limited view, endless small duties and deprivations and no certainty as to whether we are winning or not; these are the conditions of the long struggle for the victory of disinterested love. It is often the patient defence of an unnoticed corner which decides the result. The difference between the real spiritual experiences even of sanctity, and the popular notion of them, is the difference between the real private in the trenches and the glossy photograph of the same warrior, taken when he is home on leave.

Yet the whole power and life of the Invisible God, the Divine Charity itself, stands by us in the trenches. 'As ye are partakers of the suffering, so are ye of the support,' says St. Paul to the Corinthians.

UNCONDITIONAL LOYALTY

The Wisdom that came forth from the mouth of the Most High entered deeply into the common life, and there accomplished His transforming and redeeming work. We too are not to experience eternity and take up our obligations in respect of it in some exalted other-worldly region; but here and now, right down in that common life which is also dear to God, finding in our homely experience the raw material of sacrifice, turning its humble duties and relationships into prayer. Be it unto me according to Thy Word—here, where I am. Not my will but Thine be done. This is the act of oblation which puts life without condition at God's disposal; and so transforms and sacramentalizes our experience, and brings the Kingdom in.

THE ASCENT

In practice, prayer or attention to God, and purification or self-adjustment to and with Him, must proceed together. Prayer tends directly to God; mortification removes the de-orientation of desire, and concentrates our will and love on Him alone. These are the two completing aspects of one individual life; and if we think of them separately it is, merely for the sake of convenience.

This twofold progress, to and in God, is what St. John of the Cross means by the 'ascent of Mount Carmel.' And Mount Carmel is like one of those mountains which have many summits; so that each time we think we have reached our limit, we see a new height beyond us, more beautiful and more absolute in its demand; and again the glimmering Presence, the same yet ever-changing, beckons us on. Two bypaths accompany and constantly entice the mountaineer. One offers the natural life in all its fullness and charm; the other offers spiritual consolations and experiences. Both are to be avoided by the instructed climber; for at best they lead to the pleasant lower pastures of faith. The ascent to which he has been called is to the unseen summits of the Spirit; and that means the narrow way, the rock, the rope, the guide, and such a denudation of all preference and comfort, all softness, unreality and excess, as leaves him at last capable of giving all the Spirit asks, and receiving all that Spirit gives.

First, the field of normal consciousness and conduct, where the 'I' lives in contact with the world of sense, and under the constant stimulus of desire, must be submitted to the purifying power; reordered in accordance with the standards of reality. Next, the intellectual region, where the mind is always at work analysing and interpreting, must subordinate the separate findings of reason to the over-whelming certitudes of faith; and the psychic world of memory and imagination in which so much of our waking life is passed, must disclose its fugitive and approximate character over against God. Last, the will, the principle of action, and the very expression of our personal love and life, is to be cleansed of self-interest by the action of Divine Love that the whole unified being 'reformed' in faith, hope, and charity, may tend to its one objective, the incomprehensible Being of God.

THE NEED OF RETREAT

I do not mean to recommend Retreat for merely practical reasons—because it makes the effective, active Christian, more active and effective than before. I rather recommend it because it puts in the foreground and keeps in the foreground that which is, after all, the first interest of religion; the soul's relation to God. That relation is so subtle, so invisible, so deeply personal and yet so powerful—how is its delicate beauty to be savoured and its humbling influence felt, while Martha runs from the gas-stove to the scullery, listening with one ear to the loud-speaker declaiming morning prayers?

We need for that such silence and leisure as we get in Retreat; what one of the mystics called 'a rest most busy.' Then the repressed elements of our truest being can emerge and get light and air; and perhaps such a renewal of faith, hope and charity—those three virtues that are trained wholly towards God—that they may keep their heads above water when re-immersed in the torrent of the world. . . .

The object of Retreat is the same as the object of the Christian life—Sanctity—the production, fostering and maintenance of holiness. 'To sanctify,' as von Hügel was fond of saying, 'is the biggest thing out.' Now souls are sanctified by the pressure and cleansing action of the Spirit, acting through and in the events of everyday life. But in order that the action of the Spirit may produce this effect, we know that a particular disposition, outlook, temper, is required in the soul. And how is that to be produced? Perhaps most easily and directly by taking the soul from its normal preoccupations and placing it in an atmosphere and condition in which with the minimum of distraction, it can attend to and realize God. And that, in essence is a Retreat.

It is not easy under everyday conditions to learn and maintain the art of steadfast attention to God; yet no art could more certainly serve His purposes than this. 'One loving spirit sets another on fire.' The Church will win the world for Christ when—and when only—she works through loving spirits steeped in prayer.

*

VIII

SERVICE, THE ACTIVITY OF LOVE

ST. CATHARINE OF GENOA
MYSTIC AND PHILANTHROPIST

Say, did you go
Great soul and sweet,
When first his message reached your weary heart,
Far in the wilderness your Love to greet
From all mean things apart?
Not so:
But down the alleys that his footsteps trod
Between the blind, the ailing and the lame,
Steadfast in ministry you came—
Yet swift to the encounter of your God.

The hideous bed
Of utmost poverty,
The chamber of the dead,
The busy hospital; all these did see
How that you ran, bright-faced, from ecstasy
Life's dreadful wrecks to tend
And, for his sake in each acclaimed a friend.

Ah! was it these, your well-beloved guests,
Who taught you eager pain's most stern delight,
High heaven's most dear behests?
Did you surprise
Within their fevered eyes the sudden gleam
Of Paradise?
Or watching through the night
The adept of a mighty agony,
Discern as in a dream
Behind his anguished sighs,
The murmurous olives of Gethsemane?

Novice of Love, you were initiate
By helpless hands in his divine intent;
Yea, were communicate
In Life's most pure and piteous sacrament.
Remedial mercy's art
That, cruel kind,
Would wound to mend
And with deliberate smart
Probe the deep ulcers of the infected mind;
Or, greatly daring, spend
The very life-blood of the stricken soul—
This did your schooling make you to admire,
This your blessed office teach you to extol.
Thus your translucid sight
Pierced to that purging fire.

That lazar-house of light,
Where those who greatly love,
Yet know themselves impure,
Plunge in the healing flame, their charity to prove:
That sweet sharp physic joyful to endure,
And from life's sickness work the spirit's cure.

EVER-EXPANDING LOVE

IF we love God and give ourselves to Him, we must give ourselves to the whole world. Otherwise we would divide off our personal experience of God from His Greatness and Infinite Presence and turn what ought to be dedication into private enjoyment.

One of the holy miracles of love is that once it is really started on its path, it cannot stop: it spreads and spreads in ever-widening circles till it embraces the whole world in God. We begin by loving those nearest to us, end by loving those who seem farthest. And as our love expands, so our whole personality will grow, slowly but truly. Every fresh soul we touch in love is going to teach us something fresh about God.

One of the mystics said: *God cannot lodge in a narrow heart: our hearts are as great as our love.* Let us take that into our meditation and measure our prayer and service against the unmeasured generosity of God.

THE SERVICEABLENESS OF CONTEMPLATION

The ideal of the great contemplatives, the end of their long education, is to become 'modes of the Infinite.' Filled with an abounding sense of the Divine Life, of ultimate and adorable reality, sustaining and urging them on, they wish to communicate the revelation, the more abundant life, which they have received. Not spiritual marriage but divine fecundity is to be their final state. In a sense St. Teresa in the Seventh Habitation, Suso when his great renunciation is made, have achieved the quest; yet there is nothing passive in the condition to which they have come.

209

Not Galahad but the Grail-bearer is now their type: and in their life, words or works, they are compelled to exhibit that 'Hidden Treasure which desires to be found.'

'You may think, my daughters,' said St. Teresa, 'that the soul in this state (of union) should be so absorbed that she can occupy herself with nothing. You deceive yourselves. She turns with greater ease and ardour than before to all that which belongs to the service of God, and when these occupations leave her free again, she remains in the enjoyment of that companionship.'

INWARDS, UPWARDS AND OUTWARDS

The spiritual life of any individual has to be extended both vertically to God and horizontally to other souls; and the more it grows in both directions, the less merely individual and therefore the more truly personal, it will be. It is, in the truest sense, in humanity that we grow by this incorporation of the spiritual and temporal, the deeps and the surface of life; getting more, not less, rich, various and supple in our living-out of existence. Seen from the spiritual angle, Christian selves are simply part of that vast organism, the Church Invisible, which is called upon to incarnate the Divine Life in history, and bring eternity into time. Each one of us has his own place in this scheme, and each is required to fulfil a particular bit of that plan by which the human world is being slowly lifted God-ward, and the Kingdom of God is brought in. This double action—interior and ever-deepening communion with God, and because of it ever-widening, outgoing towards the world as tools and channels of God, the balanced life of faith and works, surrender and activity—must always involve a certain tension between the two movements. Nor, as St. Paul saw, should we expect the double movement to be produced quite perfectly in any one individual: not even in the saints. The body has many members, some of them a very funny shape, but each with their own job. The man of prayer and the man of action balance and complete one another. Every genuine vocation must play its part in this transformation in God of the whole complex life of man.

SYMPATHY, THE HEIGHT OF LOVE

It is often difficult to maintain our outlook on spiritual things: life is full of harassing petty details. But remember that the mark of greatness in love, is the power of being interested in tiny nothings for love's sake. Real love is homely and gentle as well as lofty; it does not put up with petty details; it enters into them. We must often bear disappointment, weakness, stupidity from those we work among. God bears those from us all the time. How often His Grace and love reach us through and in spite of our narrow ideas of Him, our cowardice and refusals. Think of His wonderful divine loving-kindness, never despising or refusing any vessel in which we try to catch and hand on the living water. After that, can we dare to be critical or impatient with the narrowness or absurdity of the little ones of Christ? Love teaches. It is by admiration and generosity we shall help and win others. Admiration is so much more humbling to receive and ennobling to give, than any criticism. Christ never criticized any but the respectable and pious: with every one else His thought went like a shaft of delight straight to something He could admire —the love of the prostitute, the meekness of the publican, the faith of the centurion, the confidence of the penitent thief—all things which irradiate and save humanity. Love looks for those first, and one reason why Christ gives us rest, is that in His presence we are bound to love—not to criticize. The humble beauties of human nature leapt out in response to Christ, and do still. How deeply He loved and admired the children, birds, flowers: entered with sympathy into every type of soul. What a passport His love and sympathy was to the very heart of the world. That sense now called brotherhood—the vivid consciousness that God is present to us in the souls of our fellows, is of the very essence of love.

CONSECRATION AND EFFECTIVENESS

There are two sides to every vocation: unconditional giving of self to the call of God . . . and the gift of power which rewards the total gift of self to God. In Christ's life we see these two movements in perfect balance. How humbly He submitted to the Will of the Father . . . and yet . . . there is always the power to intervene, to save, mould, defeat opposition, transform even the humble accidents of life. In all men and women of prayer deeply united to God, that double state exists too. That handing of self over and the mysterious power that somehow acts through self in consequence—the right word said, the right prayer prayed. But only in proportion to the self-effacement. The power, of course, is God's, not ours. One hears people say 'He (or she) is simply wonderful!' Not at all! He or she is the self-emptied channel of the only Wonderful—the Mighty God, the Everlasting Father. When we give ourselves to Him without reserve, we become points of insertion for the rescuing spirit of Love. We are woven into the Redeeming Body so that we may provide more and more channels for God. Think of St. Francis with his special selfless love for lepers and sinners; of St. Catherine of Siena saying, 'I will take your sins upon me'; of the Curé d'Ars, or Father Wain-right, of whom it was said, 'You must be either a drunkard or a criminal to know him well.' What were their lives really but this—channels for the rescuing Spirit of Love?

That deeply surrendered union with God and docility to His requirements: that power of transforming circum-stance, of exerting a pacifying, saving and compassionate action at our own cost, is an essential part of the Pattern put before us.

THE SHEEP-DOG

We offer ourselves, one way or another, to try to work for God. We want, as it were, to be among the sheep-dogs employed by the Good Shepherd. Have you ever watched a good sheep-dog at work? He is not an emotional animal. He goes on with his job quite steadily; takes no notice of bad weather, rough ground or of his own comfort. He seldom or never stops to be stroked. Yet his faithfulness and intimate communion with his master are of the loveliest things in the world. Now and then he looks at the shepherd. And when the time comes for rest, they are generally to be found together.

Let this be the model of your love.

THE TWO-FOLD LIFE

In our day the tendency to action usually obliterates the contemplative side of experience altogether: and the result is the feverishness, exhaustion and uncertainty of aim characteristic of the over-driven and the under-fed. But no one can be said to live in its fullness the life of the Spirit who does not observe a due balance between the two: both receiving and giving, both apprehending and expressing, and thus achieving that state of which Ruysbroeck said, 'Then only is our life a whole, when work and contemplation dwell in us side by side, and we are perfectly in both of them at once.' All Christian writers on the life of the Spirit point to the perfect achievement of this twofold ideal in Christ: the pattern of that completed humanity towards which the indwelling Spirit is pressing the race. His deeds of power and mercy, His richly various responses to every level of human existence, His gift to others of new faith and life, were directly dependent on the nights spent on the mountain in prayer. When St. Paul entreats us to grow up into the fullness of His stature, that is the ideal that is implied.

FULLY LIVED HUMAN LIFE

Our spiritual life to-day, such as it is, tends above all to express itself in social activities. Teacher after teacher comes forward to plume himself on the fact that Christianity is now taking a 'social form'; that love of our neighbour is not so much the corollary as the equivalent of the love of God, and so forth. . . . Yet is there in this state of things nothing but food for congratulation? Is such a view complete? Is nothing left out? Have we not lost the wonder and poetry of the forest in our diligent cultivation of the economically valuable trees; and shall we ever see life truly until we see it with the poet's eyes? There is so much meritorious working and willing; and so little time left for quiet love. A spiritual fussiness—often a material fussiness, too—seems to be taking the place of that inward resort to the fontal sources of our being which is the true religious act, our chance of contact with the Spirit. This compensating beat of the fully lived human life, that whole side of existence resumed in the word contemplation, has been left out.

RECEIVING AND GIVING

Christ gives nobody any encouragement for supposing that a mere self-cultivating sort of spirituality, keeping the home fires burning, and so on, is anybody's main job. The main job confided to His friends is the preaching of the Gospel. That is, spreading Reality, teaching it, inserting it into existence; by prayers, words, acts, and also if need be by manual work, and always under the conditions and symbolism of our contemporary world. But since we can only give others that which we already possess, this presupposes that we have got something of Reality as a living, burning fire in ourselves. The soul's two activities of reception and donation must be held in balance, or impotence and unreality will result. It is only out of the heart of his own experience that man really helps his neighbour: and thus there is an ultimate social value in the most secret responses of the soul to grace. No one, for instance, can help others to repentance who has not known it at first-hand. Therefore we have to keep the home fires burning, because they are the fires which raise the steam that does the work: and we do this mostly by the fuel with which we feed them, though partly, too, by giving free access to currents of fresh air from the outer world.

GOD'S TOOL

Contemplation, even at its highest, dearest and most intimate, is not to be for you an end in itself. It shall only be truly yours when it impels you to action: when the double movement of Transcendent Love, drawing inwards to unity and fruition, and rushing out again to creative acts, is realized in you. You are to be a living, ardent tool with which the Supreme Artist works; one of the instruments of His self-manifestation, the perpetual process by which His Reality is brought into concrete expression. . . .

The adoration to which you are vowed is not an affair of red hassocks and authorized hymn books; but a burning and consuming fire. You will find, then, that the world, going its own gait, busily occupied with its own system of correspondences—yielding to every gust of passion, intent on the satisfaction of greed, the struggle for comfort or for power—will oppose your new eagerness; perhaps with violence, but more probably with the exasperating calmness of a heavy animal which refuses to get up. If your new life is worth anything, it will flame to sharper power when it strikes against this dogged inertness of things; for you need resistances on which to act. 'The road to a Yea lies through a Nay,' and righteous warfare is the only way to a living and lasting peace.

FINDING THE THOROUGHFARE

The proposition that this quest and this achievement constitute an egotistical and 'world renouncing religion' suited only to contemplatives, is only less ridiculous than the more fashionable delusion which makes Christianity the religion of social amiability, democratic ideals and 'practical common sense.' On the contrary, the true mystic quest may as well be fulfilled in the market as in the cloister; by Joan of Arc on the battlefield as by Simon Stylites on his pillar. It is true that since human vitality and human will are finite, many of the great mystics have found it necessary to concentrate their love and their attention on this one supreme aspect of the 'will-to-live.' Hence the cloistered mystic and the recluse obeys a necessity of his own nature: the necessity which has produced specialists in every art. But the life for which he strives, if he achieves it, floods the totality of his being; the 'energetic' no less than the 'contemplative' powers. It regenerates, enriches, lifts to new heights of vision, will and love, the whole man, not some isolated spiritual part of him; and sends him back to give, according to his capability as teacher, artist, or man of action, 'more abundant life' to the surrounding world. The real achievements of Christian mysticism are more clearly seen in Catherine of Siena regenerating her native city, Joan of Arc leading the armies of France, Ignatius creating the Society of Jesus, Fox giving life to the Society of Friends, than in all the ecstasies and austerities of the Egyptian 'fathers in the desert.' That mysticism is an exhibition of the higher powers of love: a love which would face all obstacles, endure all purifications, and cherish and strive for the whole world. In all its variations, it demands one quality—humble and heroic effort; and points with a steady finger to one road from Appearance to Reality—the Mystic Way, Transcendence.

THE WILL OF THE VOICE

'Enoch walks on the hills and hears the Voice continually and has given up his will to do the Will of the Voice . . . but it took Enoch 200 years to learn to interpret the Will of the Voice.' (Bernard Shaw, 'Back to Methuselah.')

The mystic Ruysbroeck says that the Love of God enters the little but uplifted soul of man as a simple light; and then it grows and becomes a spreading light, which flows out to all in common. Now the infinite and all-creative Love of God comes into the soul of the Church in the simple light of Christ. But it has not there been transformed into the spreading light which shall redeem the whole world; it has not been fully used, fully applied . . .

Has the simple light given to us in the story of the Magdalen been generally applied to human sin? or that of the good Samaritan to the obligations of the brotherhood? . . . As to the Sermon on the Mount, it is really a series of indictments of our 'wonderful modern civilization' . . . It is needless to continue: we know quite well that our country is not a Christian one . . . that the bit of this planet for which we are responsible is not corresponding with God's nature or fulfilling His purpose. Bertrand Russell said (pointing out the danger involved in man's half-savage impulses and his growing scientific power): 'Only kindliness can save the world.' Now I do not propose . . . to reduce the pure love of God to organized kindliness. But no one can deny that living, vivid, realistic Christianity—the reign of Christ's Love in individual hearts—*does* make men . . . more than kindly. It lights the fire of supernatural charity, compassion, self-sacrifice. It turns the prose of humanitarian conduct into poetry, turns a decent attitude to our fellows into love. . . . The Christian attitude and action are only produced and appreciated by implicitly Christian souls—those whose vision of God transcends their vision of themselves and their own interests. Real kindliness, in our little half-real and dimly conscious spirits, can only emerge as the faint reflection of a Love that immeasurably exceeds and precedes our own.

If we believe that the Incarnation reveals to us the character and purpose of Absolute Love; then it becomes a great illumination of the mind as well as a stimulus to our love and will. It links our struggle . . . with God's achieved Perfection, with a Power and Spirit that will be more and more operative in us, the more fully we give ourselves to their work and ends. 'All things work together for good to them that love God.' If they do not, for us, this may have something to do with the quality of our love. The love of God demands courage and industry. It must be whole-hearted, without a hint of reserve . . . The love of God that is truly operative, is the total self-giving of our tiny wills to His will: nothing, however hard, that is really demanded, held back in the name of prudence or reasonable behaviour. Only that personal, unlimited surrender can help us . . . to interpret the Will of the Voice; to see the proportion in which our tiny notions of necessity stand to His Nature and Purpose.

MARTHA AND MARY

The demand of the Ultimate on the tiny human self immersed in history seems to be on one hand a demand for full, generous and heroic action, deliberate striving, completeness of life; and on the other, for the humble acknowledgement that the incitement to this action and food of this life come from beyond the radius of the soul. A delicate balance must be found and maintained between the creature's surrender to those mighty energies which would transform and use it, and its own initiative, its active, willed response. The Teresian collaboration between Martha and Mary is everywhere needed. As it advances, the soul becomes ever more flexible, more able to combine the uncalculating, genial life of service with a secret and austere renunciation; and the line between God's impulse and its own willed and generous action grows ever thinner, until at last a stable union between spirit and Spirit is achieved. All this will be done by different spirits in an infinity of different ways; for sanctity, human self-giving to the purposes of the Holy, means the gradual and at last perfect supernaturalizing of the special material offered to any one soul, not rigid conformity to a pious convention or the slavish imitation of a type. Included in this material are the simple daily needs of every man and woman of good will, the whole gamut of human sufferings, and renunciations, lonely study and social relationships.

CONTAGIOUS CHRISTIANS

By the quality of our inner lives I do not mean something characterized by ferocious intensity and strain. I mean rather such a humble and genial devotedness as we find in the most loving of the saints. I mean the quality which makes contagious Christians; makes people *catch* the love of God from you. Because they ought not to be able to help doing this, if you really have got it: if you yourselves feel the love, joy, peace, the utter delightfulness of the consecrated life—and this to such an extent that every formal act of worship in church is filled with the free spontaneous worship of your soul. That is what wins people above all. It raises the simplest vocal prayer, the most commonplace of hymns, the most elaborate ceremonial action to the same level of supernatural truth. People want to see and feel this in those who come to them with the credentials of religion: the joy, the delightfulness, the transfiguration of hard dull work and suffering which irradiate the real Christian life. You can't do more for any one than give them that . . . for that means real redemption, here and now, the healing of all our psychic conflicts, all our worries and resistances and sense of injustice.